Girls' Night in

CRAFT, CAKES AND COCKTAILS
FOR THE ULTIMATE PARTY

Quadrille
PUBLISHING

HANNAH READ-BALDREY

Photography by Tiffany Mumford and Verity Welstead

*This book is dedicated
to all my girls*

Since I was a little girl I have loved hosting parties, and as a midsummer baby my birthday always used to be a great excuse for a big celebration. We have two main parties every year in our house, one for my birthday and the other at Christmas. I'm so glad I have a dining room with a long table (plus the garden table tacked onto the end) where I can squeeze in up to 23 guests for a meal, shoulder to shoulder, all on random chairs from the house, garden and next door! It's a squash, but that's half the fun of it.

Naturally my friends feature predominantly in this book; I am lucky enough to have remained close to my school friends and I can honestly say that there is no one else in the world I would prefer to spend my GNI with. Some of my greatest times have been spent with my girlfriends whilst at each other's houses, watching films, eating, drinking, playing, making, gossiping and always laughing!

These nights have inspired many of my choices for the book, from the games that have been played at the many parties over the years to ideas for cocktails and food, and one friend, who shall remain nameless, even gave me tips on how to use the Showgirl Tassels that she learnt to use whilst training as a burlesque dancer!

This book will help you to get the party started before your first guest even arrives, with ideas for enchanting handmade invites and pretty decorations. There is also a gorgeous selection of craft projects for the whole group, such as the Pretty Bow Knickers or Fabulous Fabric-covered Shoes, and fantastic beauty treatments as well as stunning make-up, hair and nail techniques. Delight your guests with delicious recipes from the food and drink section, including quirky cocktails, sweat treats and savvy savouries.

The best thing about a GNI is that you don't need to splash too much cash to have a fabulous evening, and with the boys out of the picture you can have some real quality time with your girlfriends.

So the only thing you need to decide is... Who will you invite to your GNI?!

Setting the scene
SOME ETIQUETTE AND ADVICE

par·ty [pahr-tee] ;
noun, plural par·ties, adjective, verb, par·tied, par·ty·ing.
1.
a social gathering, as of invited guests at a private home, for conversation, refreshments, entertainment, etc.: a cocktail party.

Hosting a party is great fun, but sometimes it can be daunting when getting started so here are some tips.

First things first, decide whether you want your night to be an intimate soirée or a large group. Then think about who you want to invite and consider whether you think they will all get along. Don't always invite the same group of friends, it can be fun to invite girls from different groups.

Invite your guests at least a month in advance to ensure that they can make the date and put it in their diaries. I much prefer to receive an invitation in the post – it feels far more personal than a text or email, and you can't go wrong with handmade designs.

The invitation must include two important things other than the date, time and place. One, let them know which craft project you have decided on and ask them if they are happy with your choice, it is important that all your guests are pleased. Two, always add an RSVP to the invitation.

LISTS, LISTS, LISTS!
Hosting a great party is all in the planning and if there isn't a list or two knocking around you are either a party genius or unprepared. Write down all the components you will need – your decorations, craft projects, beauty treatments, make-up ideas, food, drink, games, films and music.

What to wear
You may be lulled into thinking that just because you are at home you don't need to dress up – wrong! This is a great excuse to dress up as you don't have any journey time to contend with and you may have a new outfit you want to test-drive or a pair of shoes that you can wear for a while before they begin to hurt your feet! As the host, the more effort you make, the better your party will be.

THE WEEK BEFORE
Make sure to buy all the components for your chosen craft project early, you may need to order some of the bits online so you will need to allow time for delivery. Ask your guests to bring some of the generic materials or useful equipment such as glue guns, sewing machines, fabric, scissors, etc.

You also need to decide what food and drink you will be serving and to buy the ingredients for them. Although most can be bought in the local supermarket, some of the more obscure items may need to be ordered, so it is best to do this in advance.

THE DAY BEFORE

Firstly, decide which room you want to host your GNI in: if you are making a craft project it is best to work around the kitchen table. For an evening of pampering, you will need to split your time between the bathroom and bedroom. If you are watching a movie or playing games, choose the living room. Once you have decided, make that room special by making some of the party decorations and bunting in this book.

Can you get any of the cooking done early? Lots of the recipes are designed so that you can make them all, or at least part of them, the day before.

Are you having cocktails? If so, set up a bar area by lining a small table with a bin bag and then covering with a disposable cloth to prevent the area from becoming too wet and sticky.

Are there enough seats for your guests? If not, borrow some from a neighbour or friend.

Day of the party

I love the moment right before all my guests arrive, everything is done so I have a little sip of something nice and take a minute to relax. Now, remember to have a great time and if someone offers to help, always say yes!

PERFECT PARTY CHECKLIST

* In which room will I be hosting my GNI?

* Is everything clean, tidy and welcoming?

* Do I want to decorate any particular room?

* Which craft project are we going to make and have I bought everything that we will need?

* Will I be making any of the spa treatments or testing any of the hair and make-up ideas?

* Which recipes will I be using?

* Which cocktails are we going to make?

* What music do we want to listen to?

* Are we going to play any party games?

Party
INVITATIONS

EVERY GREAT PARTY STARTS WITH AN INVITATION and first impressions really do count, so invite your guests in style with one of these gorgeous cards.

SHOE

YOU WILL NEED

26 x 13cm of patterned scrapbook card
2 sheets of 13 x 5cm scrapbook card, for edging
glue
hole punch
50cm of 5mm-wide ribbon

Fold the large sheet of card in half to create a 13cm square. The patterned side should be right side up. Trace the shoe shape on page 176 onto the card, lining up the back of the shoe with the marked foldline and cut out.

Use the template to trace and cut out the shoe edging from the smaller sheets of card. Glue the edging in place on both sides of the shoe.

Using the hole punch, make pairs of holes (about 1cm apart) where marked on the template.

Write your message inside the card. Lace up the shoes and finish with a little bow at the top.

COCKTAIL

YOU WILL NEED

2 sheets of 7 x 4cm card, in bright and pale yellow
selection of patterned scrapbook card for the straw
  and umbrella
14.5cm square of tracing paper
clear glue
cocktail stick
12 x 6.5cm pale blue card

Using the templates on page 177, cut out the lemon
slice from the bright yellow card, the lemon skin
from the pale yellow card and the straw and two
umbrellas from the scrapbook card.

To make the glass, fold the tracing paper in half.
Open up and trim 5mm off the short bottom width
and the outer long edge of one half of the paper. Fold
the tracing paper in half again and fold the excess
on the bigger half over and around the smaller half,
mitring the corner. Glue the tabs in place.

To make the lemon, glue the pale yellow skin to the
outside edge of the lemon slice. Gently add pencil
marks to indicate the segments.

To make the umbrella, add a dot of glue to the
underside of one of the patterned pieces and place
the cocktail stick on top. Place the other piece of
paper on top with patterned side facing outwards.

Glue the straw, umbrella and lemon to the top of the
pale blue card. Write your message on the back of
the card and slide into the tracing paper glass.

Fanned skirt

YOU WILL NEED

5 x 4cm plain coloured paper, for the top
15 x 6cm patterned scrapbook paper, for the skirt
A4 sheet of card (or ready-made plain cards)
glue

Using the template on page 176, cut out the girl's top
and fold in half. Make the skirt by folding the length
of patterned paper at 1cm intervals to create a fan.

To construct, fold the sheet of A4 card in half. Draw
a pair of legs, one either side of the fold.

Place the girl's top at the top of the card, lining up
the central fold with the card fold. Position the
fanned skirt underneath the bottom of the top,
pinching the skirt at the waist to create an A-line.
Once you are happy with the positioning, glue down
both sides of the skirt and then the top. Write your
message on the back.

Pompom
DECORATIONS

YOU WILL NEED

round paper lantern, 20.5cm in
  diameter
1.5 x 1.5m of felt
fabric scissors
glue gun

THESE JOYOUS PRETTIFICATIONS WILL LIGHT UP ANY ROOM! They are really simple to do and can be made the day before. Why not make them in different sizes or hang them up with colourful paper lanterns and fanned decorations for an extra wow factor?

Secure the wire structure inside the outside shell of the paper lantern according to manufacturer's instructions.

Fold the length of felt into three layers. Using a small tea cup as a template, draw around the outside onto the felt and repeat over the rest of the felt, cutting out as many circles as possible. Alternatively, use the largest circle below as your template.

To make the roses, place a dot of glue in the centre of each felt circle and fold in half to create a semicircle. Add another dot of glue to the centre of the straight side and fold the felt in half again to create quarters.

Using more dots of glue at the folded edges of felt, attach all the roses. Begin at the top of the lantern and work your way down in a spiral action. Go back and fill in any empty spaces at the end.

*NB The size of the circle and the amount of felt you will need varies depending on the size of your lantern so the larger circle on the left is just a rough guide.

YOU WILL NEED

6 sheets of A4 black card
selection of scrapbook papers
glue
selection of buttons and paper trims
3.5m of 1cm-wide black ribbon
36 mini clothes-pegs

Trace the legs on page 177 onto the black card and cut out.

Draw some outfits, such as dresses, tops and skirts, onto the scrapbook paper and cut out. Glue the top and skirt sections together, then decorate with buttons and trims, the more unique each one is the better. Glue the legs to the back of the dresses and skirts and leave to dry completely.

Hang the ribbon in your desired location and use the mini clothes-pegs to pin up the leggy bunting pieces.

MAKES
3.5M

Leggy
BUNTING

THIS LOVELY BUNTING is perfect for a GNI and is a nice
move away from the traditional triangular version.

TALKING-POINT
CRACKERS

GET THE PARTY STARTED with these cute little crackers which can be filled with personalised questions.

MAKES
1

Roll the square of card into a tube shape and glue to secure.

Write your talking point on the small piece of card and place inside the card tube. If using, also add a treat at this point.

Wrap the crepe paper around the outside of the card tubes, and secure in place with some glue, leaving both ends open.

Thread the cracker snap through the middle of the covered tube. Tie each end closed with a 15cm length of ribbon or string. Trim the ends.

Decorate with some patterned scrapbook papers if you wish.

Lay out one cracker per guest.

TALKING POINTS

* What is the strangest food you have ever eaten, and would you eat it again?

* Tell everybody what you think is your best asset, then ask them all to say what they think is your best asset.

* For everyone – if you were stranded on a desert island, what one item of make-up, one item of clothing and one food would you be unable to live without?

* If you won 15 million pounds, what would you do with it?
(None of it can go to charity!)

* Name the first boy you ever kissed – where were you and how old were you?

* If you could have been called anything, what would you have chosen?
(You can always change your name by deed poll!)

* If they were making a film of your life, which celebrity would you like to play you, and who would be the leading man?

* If you had three wishes, what would they be?

Craft Projects

I've designed this fabulous selection of girly treasures to be made over a good natter, a glass of something nice and a cake or two. There are so many divine ideas to choose from that you may have trouble picking just one. The delightful Bunting Necklace, the Bag Charm and Butterfly Masks will be easily completed in an hour or so, whereas the Pin-up Girl Tea Towel, Simple Sewn Skirt and Fabulous Fabric-covered Shoes will take a little more time. As your guests may range in crafting abilities, make sure you choose a project that suits their skills.

Pretty Bow KNICKERS

YOU WILL NEED

50cm square of silk
thin dressmaking pins
fabric scissors
2.5m of 5mm-wide elastic
1.2m of 1.5cm-wide non-fray ribbon
matching and contrasting sewing
  threads

UK WOMAN'S SIZE	MEASUREMENT
8–10	88–92cm
10–12	93–97cm
12–14	98–102cm
14–16	103–107cm
16–18	108–112cm

PATTERN GRADING

Begin by measuring your hip size. To do this, measure around your hips at the middle point of your hipbones. For a general guide, use the chart (below, left) for measurements.

The instructions here are for a UK size 12. The hip measurement for a UK size 12 is 100cm. Divide this measurement by 4 (this represents the quarters the paper pattern is split into) then add an additional 2cm for the ruching. So:

100cm (hip measurement) ÷ 4 = 25cm
25cm + 2cm (ruching) = 27cm

This means you will need to enlarge the length of the waist on the template on page 178 to 27cm. The rest of the template pieces will now be in the correct proportion. Cut out the pattern pieces.

Start by gently steaming your silk and, using thin dressmaking pins, pin the pattern pieces onto the silk. On a clean, flat table carefully cut the silk on the fold adding a 1.5cm seam allowance all the way around. Make sure not to pull the silk out of shape. Fold under and press 7mm twice along the leg and waist edges of the front and back panels to form a double hem (1). Topstitch in place with matching thread.

1

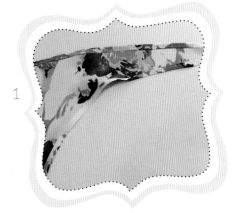

Place one of the gusset pieces together with the front panel, with right sides facing and raw edges aligned (2). Place the second gusset piece together with the front panel this time with the right side of the gusset facing the wrong side of the front and raw edges aligned. The lower edge of the front panel is now sandwiched between the two gusset pieces. Stitch together with a 1.5cm seam allowance. Open out the seams and press.

Lay the front panel and gusset with right side facing upwards. Twist the two gusset pieces so the wrong sides face upwards but the front panel stays in position (3). Place the back panel between the two gusset pieces with the right side facing upwards. Join with a 1.5cm seam allowance. Open out the seams and press.

Turn under and press the side seam allowance along the gusset edges. Topstitch these edges together.

Starting at the top corner of the front panel and stitching 1cm in from the edge, sew the elastic to the knickers using zigzag stitch in a contrasting colour sewing thread. As you stitch, gently pull the elastic to create the ruching effect. It is preferable to use a heavy foot on your machine as it's not uncommon for the zigzag stitch to move around a little. Repeat for all leg and waist edges.

To finish, tack a 30cm length of ribbon to each side edge of the front and back panels facing inwards. Turn under and press each side edge twice, then topstitch the seams to secure (4). Remove the tacking. Tie the ribbons into bows at the sides.

Memory GAME

TEST YOUR ABILITY TO REMEMBER THE MOST RANDOM OF SHOPPING LISTS.

Sit in a circle or at a table facing one another. Randomly decide who will start the game.

The first player recites: 'When I went to the shops I bought…' and adds an item to the end, i.e. '…a pair of shoes.'

The second player then repeats: 'When I went to the shops I bought a pair of shoes…' and again adds another random item to the end, i.e. '…and a banana.'

The third player then repeats: 'When I went to the shops I bought a pair of shoes and a banana…' and then adds another item to the end, i.e. '…and a spaceman.'

This continues around the circle with more items being added on each go. When a player forgets an item or says them in the wrong order, they are disqualified and the others continue until there is a winner. You can spice up the game with a forfeit like eating a spoonful of baby food, biting a chilli or taking a shot of alcohol.

TIP: Visualise all of the items being bought and it will help you to remember them!

COCKTAIL RING

YOU WILL NEED

0.8mm silver jewellery wire
wooden ring mandrel or wooden
  spoon handle (it needs to be
  slightly larger than the width of
  your finger)
cutting pliers
10cm length of 0.4mm silver
  jewellery wire
diamanté beads and crystals
flat-nosed pliers

MARILYN SAID, 'Diamonds are a girls best friend.' Well, this cocktail ring contains diamanté's, is that close enough?!

Wrap the 0.8mm wire around the mandrel three to four times. Check against the size of your finger – it should be slightly loose as the ring size will decrease as the beading is added. Cut the wire, leaving about 2.5cm of wire on either side and wrap the ends tightly around the ring shape two to three times to hold. Trim off any excess so that the wire ring is flush.

Using the piece of 0.4mm wire, tightly wrap two to three times around one of the rings joins.

Thread two beads onto the wire and wrap the wire around the ring a couple of times to secure in place. Repeat with more of the beads and crystals until you are happy with your design.

Finish by wrapping the thinner wire around on the other side of the beaded section. Trim off any excess wire and squash the sharp ends into the beads using flat-nosed pliers.

Floral
FELT FASCINATORS

MAKES 1

Before you start to decorate your fascinator, run a line of glue along the top of the flat edge of the hair comb and attach it to the underside of the fascinator base. Leave to dry whilst you make the felt flowers and leaves.

It is best to plan the design before you start making the flowers and leaves. Once you have decided on your decoration, make the petals and flowers following the steps on pages 26–7. Position the flowers on the top of the fascinator base and when you are happy with the design add some glue to the base of the flowers and leaves and press down firmly. Leave to dry, about 30 minutes.

WHERE DID YOU GET THAT HAT?
WHERE DID YOU GET THAT HAT?

I LOVE MILLINERY, ESPECIALLY AFTER CO-CREATING THE FABULOUS TABLE OF MAD HATTERS HATS FOR *EVERYTHING ALICE*, AND IT IS NOT UNCOMMON FOR YOU TO SEE A CRAZY HEADPIECE OR TWO ON ONE OF MY PHOTO SHOOTS. These beautiful fascinators are perfect for a special occasion such as a wedding or a vintage party. The technique is really quite simple but the effect is stunning.

THE FLOWERS

To make an open rose, you need two small teardrop shapes for the inside layer, three medium-sized for the middle layer and four large teardrops for the outside layer. Place a blob of glue at the base of each and pinch the sides in on themselves to form individual curved petals (1). Starting with the small petals and working up to the large, add each petal at an angle below the previous one and glue the pressed petal bases together (2). This will create a deep, open flower (3).

For a daisy, you will need to cut out five or six identical pointed oval shapes. One by one, place a small blob of glue at the base point of each petal and pinch the sides in on themselves to form a point at the end (4). Glue the sides of the petal bases together, side by side and with the fold facing inwards (5). Glue on a gem or button at the centre if desired.

For a rose, cut a 2–3cm-wide strip of felt – 5cm long for a small flower and 8cm long for a large one. Run a line of glue all the way along the long bottom edge and roll up at a slight angle so that the outer edge ends up slightly higher than the centre of the roll.

Make as many flowers as you need to cover your fascinator. Leaves are a good way to fill in small holes on your fascinator, so cut out a leaf shape, place a small blob of glue on the bottom of the flower and attach.

ROSE   DAISY

1

2

3

4

5

6

Pin-Up Girl
TEA TOWEL

Pin-Up Girl
TEA TOWEL

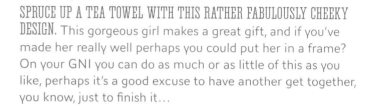

YOU WILL NEED

white paper
white tea towel, clean and ironed
dressmaker's disappearing-ink pen
light box (optional)
large embroidery hoop
selecton of embroidery threads
embroidery needle

SPRUCE UP A TEA TOWEL WITH THIS RATHER FABULOUSLY CHEEKY DESIGN. This gorgeous girl makes a great gift, and if you've made her really well perhaps you could put her in a frame? On your GNI you can do as much or as little of this as you like, perhaps it's a good excuse to have another get together, you know, just to finish it…

Using the templates on pages 178-9, trace the motifs onto your tea towel. To do this, first trace your motifs onto a sheet of paper. Then lay the tea towel over the paper and use a dressmaker's disappearing-ink pen to trace the motifs – this is much easier to do on top of a light box.

Mount the embroidery hoop, pulling the tea towel fabric taut. This will make stitching far easier.

Embroider the pattern in your chosen colours using simple backstitch. Trim off any excess threads.

TIP: Buy the tea towels from a catering shop, they are much cheaper and you can bulk buy for an embroidery based GNI.

BOOK Club

THESE BOOKS ARE SOME OF MY PERSONAL FAVOURITES AND ARE GREAT FOR DISCUSSION.
IDEALLY, THEY ALL HAVE STRONG, MEMORABLE FEMALE CHARACTERS.

THE HELP. *by Kathryn Stockett*

Set in Mississippi in 1962. Racial segregation is still practised but black maids raise white children. Centred around the experiences of Aibileen and Minny, two black maids, and Skeeter, a young, white, aspiring writer. Their lives converge over a clandestine project that will put them all at risk.

THE BOOK THIEF. *by Markus Zusak*

This book is narrated by Death and is set in Nazi Germany during the Second World War. A gravedigger's handbook is stolen by a young girl called Liesel, a life-changing act that leads to cruel twists of fate and coincidences. The ending left me weeping on the train to work!

THE LADIES NO. 1 DETECTIVE AGENCY, *by Alexander McCall Smith*

This charming book is the first in a series of 13 and you are advised to read them in order. Precious Ramotswe is Botswana's finest and one and only female private detective. A traditionally built Botswana woman, she and her assistant solve a whole manner of mysteries in unconventional and often hilarious ways.

The Crimson Petal and The White. *by Michel Faber*

Sugar is an alluring, 19-year-old whore in Victorian London. At the heart of this book is the compelling struggle of a young woman to lift her body and soul out of the gutter. This is a big, juicy, must-read of a novel that will truly delight, enthrall, provoke and entertain.

The Night Circus, *by Erin Morgenstern*

In the dead of night, 1886, a mysterious travelling circus appears out of nowhere. The Circus of Dreams is no conventional spectacle. This is about the tangled relationship between two young magicians, Celia, the enchanter's daughter, and Marco, the sorcerer's apprentice. At the behest of their shadowy masters, they find themselves locked in a deadly contest, forced to test the very limits of the imagination, and their love.

FREEZER PAPER
T-SHIRTS

YOU WILL NEED

roll of freezer paper

cotton jersey T-shirt or top, washed
 and ironed

pencil

craft knife and cutting mat

iron

old newspaper

fabric paints in various colours

old bowl

medium-sized foam paintbrush

iron-on or Hot Fix diamanté gems and
 application wand (optional)

EVER WANTED TO DESIGN YOUR OWN
T-SHIRT? Well this is an ingenious
way to create a bespoke design
without expensive screen-printing.

Pick your design, either use the motifs on page 179 or draw your own illustration onto a sheet of paper. For stars, use the motifs on page 180.

Cut a length of freezer paper that is the same width as your T-shirt. Lay the freezer paper over the top of your chosen T-shirt design shiny side down, and trace around all the elements of the design onto the dull side of the paper. Using a craft knife and cutting mat, cut the design from the freezer paper.

Position the length of freezer paper over the T-shirt – the shiny, adhesive side of the paper should be facing downwards. Once in place, press a warm iron over the paper, but do not steam. Take your time doing this as you need to make sure that all the edges are firmly stuck down, otherwise the paint will bleed.

To paint on the pattern, place some newspaper inside your T-shirt to prevent the paint from soaking through to the back. You will need to use paints that are darker than the colour of your fabric to ensure the design is defined. Pour some of your paint into an old bowl and using the foam brush, dab the paint over your cut out design. Leave to dry for at least 5 minutes. Once dry, cover with another layer of paint to ensure an even covering.

Following the manufacturer's instructions given on your paint, allow to dry fully before peeling away the freezer paper.

If you like, you can add additional iron-on diamanté jewels using an application wand to make the design extra special.

Simple
SEWN SKIRT

YOU WILL NEED

2.5cm-wide elastic, the length of your
  waist plus 1.5cm for seam allowances
fabric scissors
your chosen fabric (see instructions
  for amount)
matching thread
embroidery thread and needle (optional)

GETTING THE BASIC MEASUREMENTS RIGHT

Width If you are using a thin fabric, you will need a piece of fabric with a width that is two times your waist measurement. If you are using a thicker, heavier fabric you will only need a width that is one and a half times your waist measurement. Add an extra 5cm of seam allowance to the width of the skirt.

Length The great thing about this design is that you can make it as short or as long as you like. Use the guide below to work out your preferred skirt length and then add an extra 16.5cm for the hemline, waistband and seam allowances.

See the following page for instructions on how to calculate your exact measurements.

Mini Length
Measure from your waist to the middle part of your thigh.

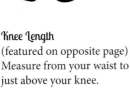

Knee Length
(featured on opposite page)
Measure from your waist to just above your knee.

Maxi Length
You may need to get one of the girls to measure this for you as you need to measure from your waist to the floor.

This does require a little maths...

The instructions given are for a knee-length skirt in a thin fabric. I have used my measurements; replace the figures with yours.

WIDTH

My waist is 71cm.
The width of my fabric should therefore be 2 x 71cm, plus 5cm for the seam allowances.
So the total width is: 147cm.

LENGTH

My waist to knee is 53.5cm.
The length of my fabric should therefore be 53.5cm, plus 5cm for the hemline, 6.5cm for the waistband and 5cm for the seam allowance.
So the total length is: 70cm.

You will therefore need to cut your fabric to a rectangle measuring 147cm wide by 70cm long.

Measure your elastic waistband by placing the elastic around your waist and gently pulling – you do not want it to be tight, you just want a bit of tension. Add 1.5cm for seam allowance and cut.

Press your fabric and cut to size following the calculations shown on the left. Fold your fabric in half lengthways with right sides facing and sew the side seam in a straight line, leaving a 2.5cm seam allowance.

With the skirt still wrong side out, turn up the bottom edge by 2.5cm and iron to crease. Fold over a further 2.5cm and carefully stitch the hem in place.

To create the waistband, fold down the top edge of the fabric by 2.5cm and press. Fold over another 4cm and press. Start to stitch about 5mm from the bottom of the folded edge to create a channel between the top edge and the stitching. Start to thread the elastic through the channel and then continue stitching. Repeat this method, stitching a little then threading through more of the elastic. Make sure you do not stitch any of the elastic to the skirt. Once you have stitched almost the whole way around, stitch the two ends of the elastic together with a 1.5cm overlap and stitch the rest of the channel closed.

Using a very hot iron, steam press the length of the skirt. Steam the ruched waistband flat. Leave plain or embroider the skirt using one of the motifs on page 180–1. Use backstitch and simple long straight stitches for the embroidery.

BEFORE I WROTE THIS BOOK, I ASKED ALL MY GIRLFRIENDS WHAT ONE ITEM THEY WOULD LIKE ME TO TEACH THEM TO MAKE. The resounding answer was clothing. So I came up with this gorgeous, versatile skirt which can be made to your bespoke length and can be kept simple or embellished with a selection of embroidered motifs.

PHOTO Booth!

EVER FANCIED SEEING WHAT YOU WOULD LOOK LIKE WITH A COMEDY MOUSTACHE OR A PAIR OF DAME EDNA SPECKS? Well, this could be the game for you; I mean what could be more fun than playing dress-up with the girls? Nothing I tell you!

The props can be made beforehand or with the girls.

Transfer the templates on page 181 onto card and cut out. If you like, draw some of your own and decorate these props with sequins and jewels.

Use the glue gun to firmly attach a doweling rod to the back of each prop. Lay out on a table or place in a vase for easy access.

YOU WILL NEED

selection of card, in different colours
  and patterns
hot-glue gun
sequins and decorations
40cm length of 1cm doweling rod,
  one for each prop

a digital camera
tripod (optional)
a plain wall or a piece of fabric hung
  over a door
laptop (optional)
photo printer (optional)

The GAME

The game is simply who can come up with the best combination of props and facial expressions. Each girl can dress up and take a photo. You may find this easier if the camera is on a tripod, which also enables you to take group photos.

It is also great to be able to see the photos immediately, so load the photos onto a laptop. It will be easier to judge them this way and what's-more, you can print them as a memento of your GNI!

Giggles
GUARANTEE

BUNTING NECKLACE

YOU WILL NEED

fabric scissors
10 scraps of leather or leatherette, each
  in different, complementary colours
leather hole punch
64cm length of gold chain
flat-nosed pliers
2 jump rings
gold clasp

Cut 10 leather triangles using the shape below. Using the leather hole punch on the 3mm setting and following the markings on the pattern, make two holes in the corners of the shorter side of the triangle (1) on each triangle (2).

Thread the gold chain from front to back through one of the holes and from back to front back out through the other. The middle section of chain should sit behind the bunting piece (3). Repeat this method with the remaining triangles, arranging the colours as you go.

Use pliers to open the jump rings and thread them through the ends of the chain. Place the clasp attachment on one of the open rings and close both jump rings using flat-nosed pliers.

THIS IS SUCH A SIMPLE AND EFFECTIVE NECKLACE. It looks like it has come straight out of a contemporary jewellery shop.

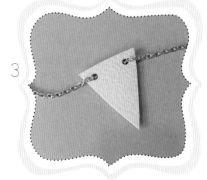

YOU'RE GOING TO LOVE THIS LUXURY
MAKE-UP BRUSH ROLL.
It provides you with somewhere
to cleanly store and easily
transport your brushes, as
well as looking fabulously
professional. But the best thing
has to be that the roll is made
from only one piece of fabric!

MAKES 1

MAKE-UP
BRUSH ROLL

Press your fabric until there are absolutely no creases. Lay the fabric in front of you widthways across the wrong side of the fabric: right side down and with one of the shorter edges nearest to you. Using a soft pencil, mark three lines, the first 20cm from the top, the second 26cm below the first and the third 15cm below the second.

Fold the fabric along the two outer lines with right sides together (at the first and third foldlines). Press the folds. Pin the side edges together and stitch along the edges leaving a 1cm seam allowance. Turn the fabric right side out, using a pencil to push out the corners. Press flat. Next, press under the seam allowance between the two 'pockets'. Then fold along the remaining pencil line (the second foldline) to enclose the raw edges and pin the sides together to form the brush pocket. Topstitch along the sides of the pocket.

To make the individual brush pockets, simply stitch straight lines along the front pocket. This can be done according to the sizes of your brushes – for my roll I have sewn five 4cm-wide pockets, four 5cm and one 6cm, with sizes ascending from left to right.

Press the ribbons in half lengthways, with wrong sides together. Fold under by 1cm along each long edge and press again. Turn in each end and stitch all the way around the edge of the ties.

To finish, stitch one tie to the back of the right-hand side of the roll, 4cm in from the edge and just above the pocket line. Repeat with the other tie on the other side of the roll. Fill with your favourite brushes and roll up.

YOU WILL NEED

iron
piece of heavyweight fabric 70cm long
   x 48cm wide, (for example linen,
   denim, canvas or a heavy cotton)
soft fabric pencil
50cm of 1cm-wide matching ribbon

ULTIMATE
Top 20 Chick Flicks!

A GREAT MOVIE IS ALWAYS WONDERFUL FUN! WHY NOT BE REALLY GIRLY AND HAVE A CHICK FLICK MARATHON, OR ASK YOUR GUESTS TO DRESS UP AS CHARACTERS FROM THE FILM!

1. Dirty Dancing
2. Titanic
3. Pretty Woman
4. Steel Magnolias
5. Bridesmaids
6. Ghost
7. Clueless
8. Sister Act and Sister Act 2
9. Bridget Jones's Diary
10. Beaches
11. Thelma and Louise
12. Moulin Rouge
13. Romeo and Juliet
14. Step Up
15. Erin Brockovich
16. The Holiday
17. Devil Wears Prada
18. An Affair to Remember
19. Notting Hill
20. Some Like it Hot

Cute CLUTCH BAG

YOU WILL NEED

fabric scissors
two 25 x 20cm pieces of patterned
 fabric, in contrasting colours
two 20 x 15cm pieces of matching
 patterned fabric
matching thread
iron
9cm bobble top purse clasp (see
 the Directory on page 185)
super-glue
pair of small scissors
pliers

Using the templates on page 182, cut out two outer shells from the larger fabric, and two lining pieces from the smaller.

Pair up the lining fabric, with right sides facing, and stitch around the sides and bottom leaving a 5mm seam allowance. Leave the top section open. Repeat for the outer shell. Turn the lining shell right side out.

Tuck the lining into the outer shell; the wrong sides of both fabrics should be visible. Pin the small tucks along the top where marked on the pattern. Sew the top edge, leaving a small opening.

Turn the fabrics right side out through the opening. Lay the lining flat in the outer shell and press. Fold in the seam allowance along the opening and close by topstitching as close to the edge as possible.

To add the clasp, run a line of super-glue along the inside of one of the metal sides. Line up the handle and the top of the bag so that the fabric sits centrally. Starting at one end, use the small scissors to poke the edge of the fabric into the metal. This can be fiddly so take your time. Repeat for the other side. Use pliers to clamp the edges down and leave to dry fully before using.

THIS SCRUMPTIOUS CLUTCH IS INSPIRED BY A BAG I MADE MY GIRLFRIENDS WHEN I WAS 16. My mum had brought home an old sample book of curtain fabrics and I was immediately inspired to get making. They loved them so much that two of my friends, Becca and Jess, still have and use them to this day!

Mini-me DOLL

YOU WILL NEED

fabric scissors
20 x 30cm of flesh-coloured cotton, for face and arms
A4 sheet of felt, for hair
20 x 40cm of patterned fabric, for body
30cm square of patterned fabric, for legs
A4 sheet of felt, for shoes and collar
black, white, blue, green, brown, red and pale pink fabric pens
matching thread and needle
bag of soft toy stuffing
buttons, ribbons and trims

Using the templates on pages 182–3, cut from the flesh fabric: one head and four arms. Cut from the hair felt: one back of the head and front hair section. Cut from the body fabric: two body shapes. Cut from the leg fabric: four legs. Cut from the remaining felt: two collars and four shoe pieces.

Frame the front hair over the flesh-coloured head. Before you start stitching use the pens to draw facial features onto the flesh cotton, this way you can easily replace the piece if you are unhappy with the drawing! I have used red for lips, black for eyelashes and nose, brown for eyebrows and white and blue for the eyes. Use your finger to dab on some pink for the cheeks.

Frame the front hair piece around the face and stitch in place, topstitching 5mm in from the edge of the hairline.

Stitch the collars to the body pieces. Fold under 5mm along the bottom edge of each body piece and press. Stitch the neck of the face piece and the back of head to the correct body pieces, with the overlap on the wrong side.

To make up the legs, tack a shoe to the foot of each leg. Right sides facing, pair the legs. Stitch 5mm in from the edge, leaving the tops open. Turn right side out. Fill with stuffing, packing evenly using the round-ended handle of a wooden spoon.

Repeat the method with the arms. Position the arms, facing downwards, at the top of the back body piece and tack in place.

Place the head and body pieces together with right sides facing. Stitch around the outside edge, incorporating the upper arms and leaving the hem of the dress open. Turn right side out, then stuff.

Position the legs between the layers at the hem of the dress. Topstitch closed, close to the hem.

Plait together three 15cm x 1cm strips of hair felt, securing the ends with a few stitches. Position the plait on the head and use a few stitches to set in place.

Customise your lovely doll to become more like you by adding buttons, bows or even a mini version of your favourite necklace!

HERE YOU HAVE THE OPPORTUNITY
TO MAKE A GORGEOUS MINI VERSION
OF YOURSELF! Once she has been
made you can sit her with her
friends and see if she is as good-
looking as the original!

Guess Who GAME

FOR 3 OR MORE

THIS IS THE BEST GUESSING GAME IN THE WORLD!
The aim is to find out who you are before anyone else, so watch your friends squirm with frustration!

Everybody writes the name of a familiar famous person onto card or a sticky note and, making sure that they can't see what you have written, stick it to the forehead of the person to your left.

Randomly decide who starts the game.

Each player in turn asks a question in an attempt to decipher who they are. The other players can only answer 'yes' or 'no'. If the answer is 'yes' the player asks another question, if it is 'no' move to the next player. The first person to correctly guess wins.

YOU WILL NEED

pen, for each player
piece of card or sticky note, for
    each player

Silhouette
LAMPSHADES

YOU WILL NEED

plain, light-coloured lampshade
white card, standard or printable
craft-mount permanent spray adhesive
 or other spray adhesive

Use the templates on page 183 or draw your own
motifs. Scan the motifs into your computer and print
out, or trace them onto the card.

Cut out the motifs and, in a well-ventilated room,
carefully attach to the inside of the lampshade using
the spray adhesive. Position so that there is a good
amount of space around each pattern. Leave to dry
for at least 10 minutes before mounting onto a lamp.

THESE DESIGNS CAST FABULOUS SHADOWS ACROSS THE WALL AND LOOK ESPECIALLY GREAT IN A LIVING ROOM OR CHILD'S BEDROOM. This is a very simple yet highly effective make that can be made with ease and in a short amount of time – making them the ideal project for a craft novice. If the girls have an old lampshade that they want to spruce up then get them to bring it over, otherwise just buy in a few.

RAGGED HEART GARLAND

 MAKES 1

Shape the shorter length of wire into a heart shape and make the two ends flush by wrapping the wire around itself.

Wrap the longer length of wire loosely around the wire heart, continuing around the heart until the whole length has been used to wrap. You want to create gaps and loops when doing this that will allow you enough space to attach strips of fabric (1).

Cut your chosen fabric into 2cm-wide strips, then cut these into 10cm lengths. Thread these strips halfway into the gaps of the wire heart frame (2). They will not move as you add more so there is no need to knot them (3). Continue around the heart – the more fabric you add, the better it will look. Once all the fabric has been added, trim so that the strips are a regular length.

Tie a ribbon around the top of the heart and hang from a door.

MAKE THIS HEART WITH LOVE; IT LOOKS GORGEOUS HUNG FROM A DOOR IN THE BEDROOM OR LIVING ROOM. The process is very simple, so a great project for varying levels of skills.

1

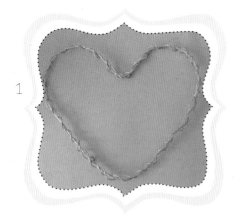

2

3

BUTTERFLY
BAG CHARM

YOU WILL NEED

chopping board

cling film

selection of Fimo oven clay (I used 602
  glitter purple, 502 glitter green, 112
  glitter gold and 37 blue)

rolling pin

butterfly, daisy and rose leaf cutter sets

baking tray

metal skewer

jewellery cutters and pliers

1m of 4mm chain, in antique
  copper

bag of 7mm jump rings, in antique
  copper

bag charm clips, in antique copper

Cover a chopping board with a piece of cling film. You will need to use a new sheet of cling film for each colour of Fimo clay – this will protect the surface of the board from staining and will ensure that the colours remain separate. A colour at a time, use a rolling pin to flatten a piece of Fimo clay until it is about 2mm thick. Clean your rolling pin between each colour.

Using the sets of cutters, carefully cut out your desired shapes and place onto the baking tray. Use the skewer to make a hole in a corner of each butterfly shape, the centre of each daisy and the base of each leaf, so that you can thread through the jump rings once the clay has hardened.

Place in the oven and bake according to the manufacturers instructions. Remove from the oven and leave to cool.

Once cool, use the jewellery cutters to cut the chain into a variety of lengths, the shortest around 6cm and the longest 10cm. You will need a length of chain for each of your Fimo charms. Thread a jump ring through the end of one chain and the hole of a charm and close the ring using pliers. Thread another jump ring through the other end of the chain and the bag charm clip and close using pliers. Repeat with the remaining charms.

Clip to the side of your bag and wear with pride!

THIS IS A GREAT WAY TO BRING INDIVIDUALITY TO YOUR BAG; THESE CHARMS HAVE FAST BECOME A SOUGHT-AFTER FASHION ACCESSORY IN RECENT YEARS. They are made using Fimo, an oven-hardening modelling clay that comes in all colours of the rainbow and in a variety of finishes.

Alphabet CHARM BRACELET

YOU WILL NEED

length of 4mm gold chain
cutting pliers
100 alphabet beads (about
  15–20g)
100 25mm-long gold headpins
round-nosed pliers
flat-nosed pliers
2 jump rings
gold clasp

THIS BRACELET IS GREAT FOR ASSEMBLING OVER A BIT OF A GOSSIP; by the end of making one you will know from A–Z what's going on with your girls!

Use a piece of string to measure loosely around your wrist to determine your preferred length of chain. Cut your gold chain to size using cutting pliers.

Thread one alphabet bead onto each headpin (1) and use the round-nosed pliers to make a loop of wire just above the bead (2). Snip away the excess length using the cutting pliers, cutting close to the end of the loop but leaving a small gap to help loop onto the links of the bracelet.

Hook them onto the chain (3) and tighten the loop of the alphabet bead using flat-nosed pliers. Add at least two bead loops to a single link in the chain, but the more you are able to build up on the individual links of the chain the better it will look.

Using round-nosed pliers, open the jump rings and attach one to each end of the chain. Hook the clasp attachment onto one of the jump rings and carefully close both rings using the flat-nosed pliers. This should create a secure and solid bracelet.

Drawing
WHISPERS

YOU WILL NEED

sheet of A4 paper, for each player
a different colour pen or pencil, for
each player

Ideally, everybody should be sat around a table or have something to lean on.

Fold the sheets of paper in half widthways, then in half again.

In the top section of every sheet each player must secretly write down a well-known saying on the paper, i.e. 'there are plenty more fish in the sea' or 'the black sheep of the family'.

Everybody should now pass their piece of paper to the person on their right. This person must memorise the saying and turn the paper so that the writing is to the back, but make sure nobody

else can see what it says. On the section now at the top they must draw their version of the saying; the more detail the better.

Once finished, everybody should pass the paper to the person on their right. This person must then interpret what the drawing is (without seeing the folded-over saying), fold the drawing to the back and write down their version on the next blank quarter.

The notes are then passed to the right again, and the final person needs to draw their version of the saying in the final section. The sheet of paper is then returned to the person who originally came up with the saying, and the saying and drawings are revealed!

FOR 4 OR
MORE
PLAYERS

Fabulous
FABRIC-COVERED SHOES

YOU WILL NEED

pair of shoes with patent or
  plastic coating
6 sheets of A4 paper
pencil
scissors
fabric scissors
50cm square of fabric
paintbrush
PVA glue
canvas varnish spray
trims, bows, ribbon and buttons,
  to decorate

FOR ALL YOU CHOO ADDICTS OUT THERE,
here's a simple and fun technique
to transform a pair of old shoes or
cheap heels. It is easy for all and
totally addictive.

You will need to make new pattern pieces for each pair of shoes.

Make sure your shoes are clean, dry and all stickers are removed.

Lay your first shoe on its side on top of a sheet of paper. Using a pencil, draw around the outside edge (1). As you draw, you will need to roll the shoe back so that you incorporate the top of the heel and roll forward to ensure you get as much of the toe as possible. Cut out. Repeat with the other side of the shoe.

To make the toe pattern, lay half a piece of paper over the toe and scrunch it over the tip. Snip around the inner curve of the shoe and fold in (2). Cut out. Repeat for the second shoe.

Pin these pattern pieces to the fabric and cut out, adding an extra 1.5cm along the top edges of the shoe pattern (this will be folded into the inside of the shoe to create a flush edge). Make small notches in the seam allowance of the toe piece along the curve.

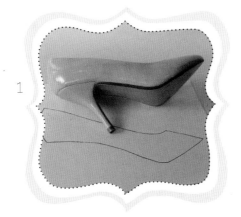

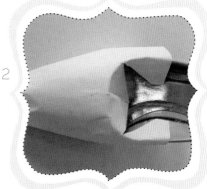

Starting on one side of the shoe, use a paintbrush to coat the side in slightly watered down PVA glue (3). Place the fabric over the shoe and paint the PVA over the top. Pull into place, the fabric should match up with the bottom seam and the seam allowance should fold over the top (4). Repeat on the other side and the toe.

To decorate the heel, cut the remaining fabric into small strips, about 1cm x 4cm. Coat the heal with PVA and add strips of fabric (5). Make sure you don't leave any gaps.

Repeat this method with the second shoe and leave both to dry.

Once dry, spray with varnish and again leave to dry.

Use a glue gun to decorate with your chosen accessories – I have attached a bow to the front of my shoes (6).

MUSIC *Playlist*

Here Come The Girls
ERNIE K DOE

Single Ladies (Put A Ring On It)
BEYONCE

Wannabe
SPICE GIRLS

Material Girl
MADONNA

Girls Just Wanna Have Fun
CYNDI LAUPER

Respect
ARETHA FRANKLIN

Doo Wop (that thing)
LAURYN HILL

I Wanna Dance With Somebody
WHITNEY HUSTON

Walking on Sunshine
KATRINA AND THE WAVES

Whatta Man
SALT-N-PEPA

My Lovin'
EN VOGUE

Doin' The Do
BETTY BOO

Buffalo Stance
NENEH CHERRY

You Don't Love Me
THE HOLLYWOOD BAND

Independent Woman
DESTINY'S CHILD

It's Raining Men
THE WEATHER GIRLS

She Works Hard For The Money
DONNA SUMMER

Hit Me With Your Best Shot
PAT BENATAR

Sisters Are Doin' It For Themselves
EURYTHMICS

Just A Girl
NO DOUBT

I'm Coming Out
DIANA ROSS

Beautiful
CHRISTINA AGUILERA

THIS IS AN ESSENTIAL PART OF ANY PARTY,
so get your girls in the mood with some
themed songs. Here is a selection of mine,
but if you want to listen for free to my full
playlist go to: www.girlsnightinbook.com.

Butterfly MASK

YOU WILL NEED

28 x 22cm of black 3mm-thick card
craft knife and cutting mat
old newspaper
paintbrush
PVA glue
glitter in assorted colours, to decorate
gems and sequins, to decorate
glue gun
hole punch
80cm of narrow ribbon

EVERYBODY LOVES DRESSING UP AND
THESE GLAMOROUS MASKS MAKE A
GREAT ONE TO SHOW OFF WITH. You
can cut out the basic mask pattern
beforehand to save time, or just get
the girls to do all the work!

Transfer the butterfly mask template on page 184 onto the sheet of card. Place the card on the mat and use the craft knife to cut around the mask. Gently score down the centre line marked on the template, do not cut.

To decorate, place the mask on some old newspaper, paint all over with PVA glue and cover with the glitter. Give the mask a good shake and re-use the excess glitter by folding the newspaper in half and carefully pouring it back into the container.

Allow the mask to dry in a warm place for 10–15 minutes, or until the glitter is dry to the touch. Attach the gems and sequins using a glue gun.

Use a hole punch to make a hole in the top, outer corner of each side of the mask, as marked on the template. Thread a 40cm length of ribbon through one side of the mask. Tie the end that appears at the front of the mask into a neat knot to secure. Repeat with the remaining 40cm length of ribbon on the other side.

MONOGRAMMED
FABRIC-COVERED BOOKS

MAKES 1
COVER

patterned fabric (see below for how to
  work out how much fabric you will
  need for each book)
long ruler
dressmaker's disappearing-ink pen
fabric scissors
matching thread
embroidery hoop (optional)
embroidery thread, in a contrasting
  colour to your fabric (optional)

WIDTH
4 x the width of the front cover +
the spine + 2cm seam allowance.

HEIGHT
Height of the book + 4cm
seam allowance.

BE THE ENVY OF YOUR BOOK CLUB WITH THIS PERSONALISED COVER.
This is a great way to spruce up and protect a book or
create a gift for someone. You can cover hardback novels,
notebooks, photo albums and diaries…

Press your fabric and lay flat on a table, right side down. Measure
the size of your book in millimetres for accuracy and work out
how much fabric you will need using the calculations on the left.
Use the ruler and pen to draw the rectangle required. Draw the
spine in place in the centre of the rectangle and the cover shape
to each side of it.

Cut out the rectangle. Press under a 1cm seam allowance all the
way around each edge. Topstitch to create a neatened edge.

If you would like to add a monogram to your book cover, do it
at this stage. Place your initials on the front of the book cover.
Use a dressmaker's pen to sketch the letters on the right side of
the fabric. If desired, draw other small flowers (or leaves) and
encircling stems around the initials. Mount the embroidery area
of the fabric onto an embroidery hoop, making sure it is pulled
taut. Use simple satin stitches for the intitials, straight stitches for
flowers, and backstitches for leaf outlines and stems.

Take the fabric out of the hoop and press. Lay the fabric on
the table right side up, then fold over both sides past the cover
outline, lining up the neatened edges with the spine marks and
pin. Stitch a 1cm seam allowance along the top and bottom,
creating two pockets. Turn the fabric right side down and press.

Slip the embroidered cover onto your book by folding back the
book covers.

Mr Centipede
BROOCH

MAKES 1

YOUR SUPER GLAMOROUS LITTLE FRIEND will sit perfectly with any designer blouse, jacket or top. This creation has been inspired by some of the world's most fashionable jewellery makers. Made with diamanté crystal beads, Mr Centipede will catch a lot of attention, so don't get jealous!

Using cutting pliers, cut a 15cm length of the 8mm wire. Make a small closed loop at the end using round-nosed pliers.

Thread on all your green diamanté beads, and then add the clear bead. Bend the wired beads into a loose S-shape.

Close the top of the wire by making another small loop at the end, leaving the beads a little loose to allow space to incorporate the legs. Cut away any excess wire. Push both loops flat against the ends of the beads so that they don't stick out.

To make the legs, cut five 10cm lengths of the 4mm wire. Take your time as this is fiddly. Thread a gold bead onto the wire and hold 1cm from the end. Twist the end of the wire back on itself and around the main length of the wire, holding the bead in place. Thread enough beads to cover about 6cm of the wire. Leave 5mm of the wire clear and add another bead. Hold the bead in place and twist the wire back on itself to close as before. Cut away the excess wire. Repeat with the remaining lengths of wire.

For each leg, split the beads in half, pushing them towards each end to leave a gap in the middle. Wrap this empty section once around one of the gaps between the green diamanté beads and repeat with the remaining legs.

Use a glue gun to attach the brooch bar to the underside.

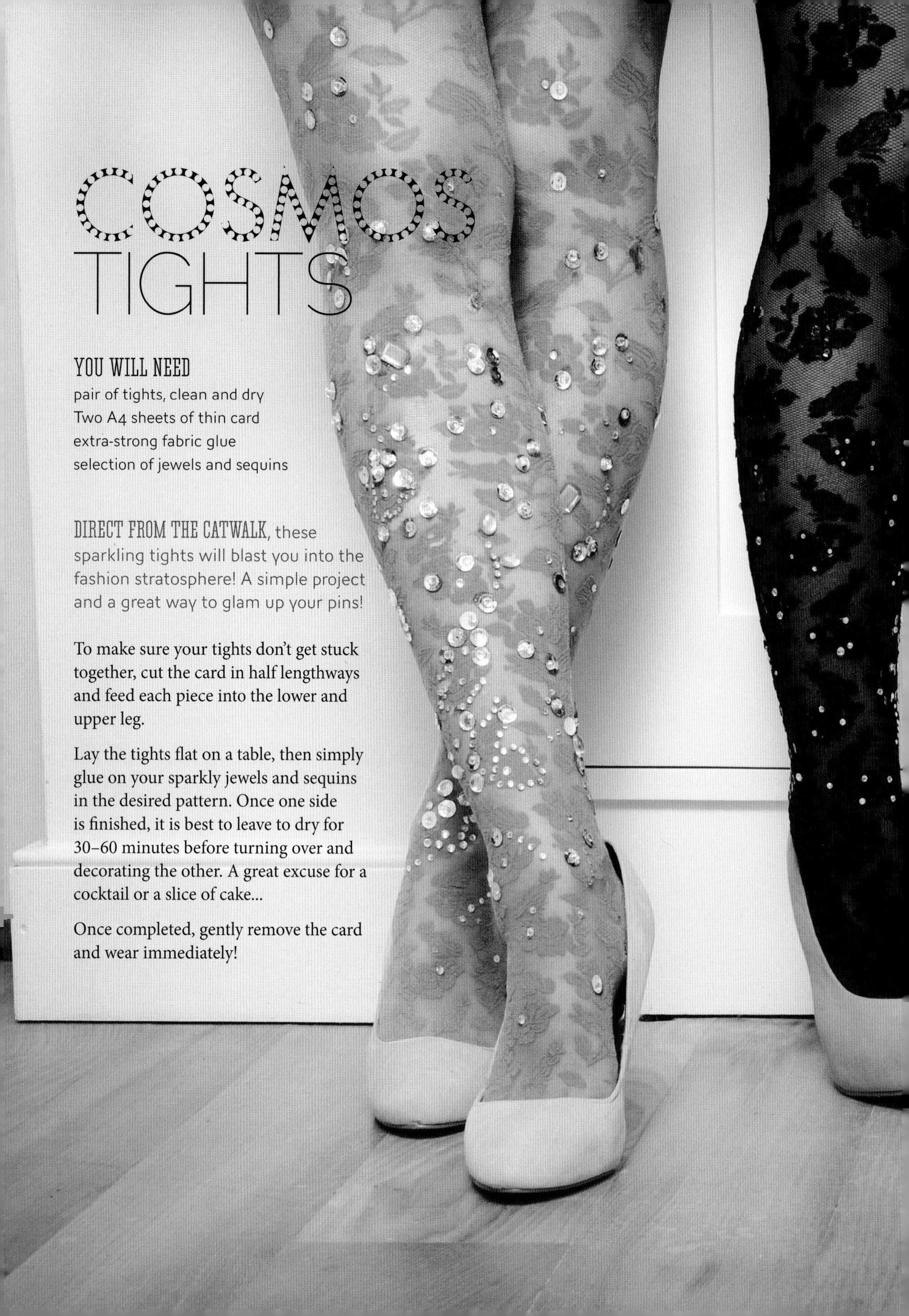

COSMOS TIGHTS

YOU WILL NEED

pair of tights, clean and dry
Two A4 sheets of thin card
extra-strong fabric glue
selection of jewels and sequins

DIRECT FROM THE CATWALK, these
sparkling tights will blast you into the
fashion stratosphere! A simple project
and a great way to glam up your pins!

To make sure your tights don't get stuck
together, cut the card in half lengthways
and feed each piece into the lower and
upper leg.

Lay the tights flat on a table, then simply
glue on your sparkly jewels and sequins
in the desired pattern. Once one side
is finished, it is best to leave to dry for
30–60 minutes before turning over and
decorating the other. A great excuse for a
cocktail or a slice of cake...

Once completed, gently remove the card
and wear immediately!

*NB TIGHTS
TO BE WORN
WITH HEELS
only

NOW THIS IS WHAT I CALL A CRAFT PROJECT! This is great if the girls are feeling a little naughty, and perfect for a hen night. One of my friends in this book trained as a burlesque dancer, and she gave me some advice on how to twirl! Why not bring out your inner diva and make a pair!

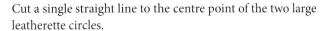

SHOWGIRL *Tassels*

YOU WILL NEED

fabric scissors
2 circles of leatherette,
 7cm in diameter
2 small tassels
glue gun
2 circles of leatherette,
 2.5cm in diameter
1m of sequin trim
double-sided body tape

Cut a single straight line to the centre point of the two large leatherette circles.

Thread the back of the tassel through the split so that the tassel sits in the centre of the circle. The back of the tassel should be at the back of the leatherette. Hold in place. Create a cone shape by overlapping 2cm of the leatherette and glue in place (1).

Turn the cone over and glue the smaller circle of leatherette over the end of the tassel, to create a flush back (2).

Turn the cone back over and attach the sequin trim; starting from the centre and working around the tassel, glue the sequins in a spiral all the way to the outer edge (3). Trim away any excess. Repeat the process for the other tassel.

Stick a triangle of body tape to the back of each tassel. Stick onto your nipple and press down to secure. You can do this over a tight-fitting top if you are feeling a little shy!

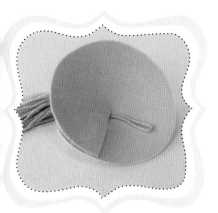

2

3

Boudoir Beauty

This section contains a whole range of wonderful treats for pampering you and your friends. Why not start with one of the homemade spa treatments, such as the relaxing Avocado and Banana Face Mask, invigorating Lemon and Vodka Foot Soak or the indulgent Lavender Salt Hand Scrub. Then try out the stunning hair and make-up ideas that were devised with the help of my close friend and expert celebrity make-up artist Fiona Fletcher, finishing the look with one of the beautiful nail designs created by rising star Lucy Pearson.

French PLAIT

I LOVE A GOOD FRENCH PLAIT, it has the perfect look of effortless chic. Either practise this look on yourself in the mirror or try it out on one of the girls. Once mastered, you will never go back to a plain old plait!

Suitable for all hair types.

1 Using a comb, part the hair to one side. If you are a novice, wet the hair with a little water as it gives it some extra grip.

2 Split the top section of the heavier weighted side of hair into three sections and begin to plait.

3 As you plait around the side of the head, take a little hair from the main bulk and add it to alternate sections of the plait.

4 Making sure you keep the plait tight to your head, plait diagonally across the back of your head continuing to add all the remaining loose hair in sections as before.

5 Once your plait has reached all the way around to the other side of your head, use a classic plait to finish to the ends of the hair.

6 Secure with a small hair band and cover with a little hair spray to hold in place.

YOU WILL NEED

comb
water spray (optional)
hair band
firm-hold hair spray

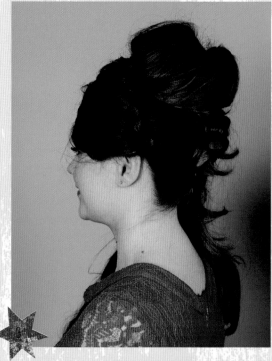

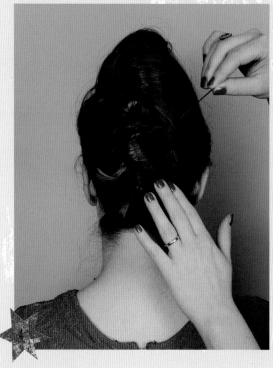

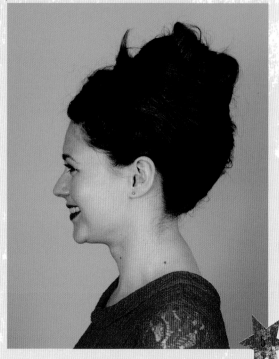

MODERN WRAP
Beehive

A FEW YEARS AGO FOR A HEN DO, I DRAGGED EVERYONE TO THE SALON TO GET A BEEHIVE. We all came out looking like *Ab Fab*'s Patsy and by the end of the evening felt like her too! This version of a Beehive really isn't as complicated as you might imagine, so give it a go!

Not suitable for fine or short hair.

1 Make sure your hair is brushed and completely dry; it helps if it is a little dirty.

2 Separate the top and the bottom of the hair into two sections. Pin the top section up out of the way. Back-comb the bottom section.

3 Split into two again and pin the top section out the way. Tightly twist the bottom section up and away from the base of the neck. This can look a little messy, but don't worry as this will make it look more modern. Unclip the other section of back-combed hair and create a large bun on the top of your head; this will add the necessary height.

4 Secure with pins.

5 Using the front section of smooth hair, wrap neat sections around the bun in different directions to disguise it. Pin the hair in place as you go and spray with hair spray to secure.

TIP: Add mousse to your hair before blow-drying to help hold the structure.

YOU WILL NEED

comb or hairbrush
short hairpins, that match
your hair colour
maximum-hold hair spray

VINTAGE ROLL

THIS VINTAGE ROLL IS A LOOK I WEAR A LOT AND I OFTEN GET ASKED HOW I HAVE DONE IT. It looks complicated but it is in fact super easy! For some reason no one ever believes me, so here is the proof in the pudding!

You will need shoulder-length hair or longer, and normal to thick hair.

1 Blow-dry or iron your hair straight. Brush your hair into a deep side parting.

2 Take the front section of the heavier side of the parting and lightly back-comb.

3 Twist this section of hair up and away from your face, ensuring the top is left with a slight lift. Pin into position towards the back of your head.

4 You now need to twist the rest of your hair around your head. Starting on the heavier side of your parting, take the front-most section of hair and start to twist towards the base of your neck. Keep the hair tight to your head and as you twist add more sections of your hair to the roll.

5 Continue to neatly twist the hair following along the line of your hairline until you have incorporated all of your hair and have reached the front of the other side of your head.

6 Turn the loose ends of your hair up and back in on itself and tuck any excess into the body of the roll. Secure by pinning into place – you may need to use quite a few pins to do this – and fix with some hair spray.

TIP: You will need to add a foam roll if you have fine hair.

YOU WILL NEED

hairbrush
long hairpins that match
   your hair colour
maximum-hold hair spray

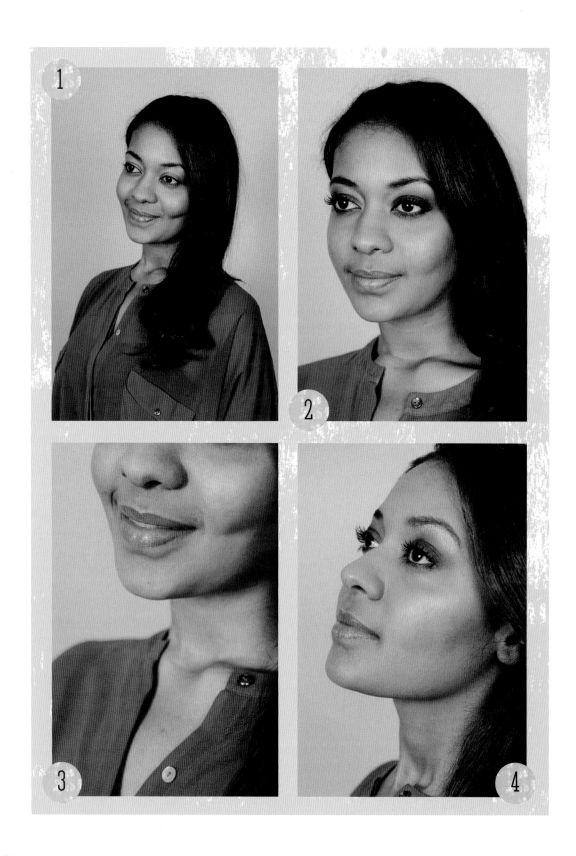

Smouldering
EYES

THIS SEXY LOOK REALLY BRINGS OUT YOUR EYES.
Be careful not to make it too heavy,
as this will have the opposite effect!

1 Evenly apply the foundation to your entire face and add a little pink blusher to the apple of your cheeks.

2 Using a purple palette to enhance the eyes, brush the dark shade on the outer edge of the eyelid, the medium shade on the inner eyelid and socket line and add a pale pink dusting under the eyebrows. Draw a pencil line close to the lashes along the top lid and smudge very gently along the lower lashes. Liberally apply mascara. Using tweezers, add the full and spiky false eyelashes.

3 Apply a little gloss to your lips to add a subtle sheen.

4 Add a healthy glow to your cheeks with a dusting of shimmer brushed above your cheekbones.

YOU WILL NEED

liquid foundation
pink blusher
eye shadow in dark purple,
    medium purple and pale pink
black pencil eyeliner
black mascara
set of full false eyelashes and
    eyelash adhesive
pink tinted lip-gloss
shimmer highlighter

CLASSIC
Vintage

APPEAR EFFORTLESSLY TIMELESS WITH THIS
VINTAGE LOOK. Take a leaf out of Marilyn's
book and go for a super glamorous
bright red lippy.

1 Evenly apply the foundation to your entire face and add a little
blusher to the apple of your cheeks.

2 Brush eye shadow over the eye socket. Using the liquid eyeliner,
draw a fine line across the top eyelid close to your eyelashes and
add a sexy feline flick at the outer edges.

3 Add a good amount of mascara to your lashes before using
tweezers to apply the strip of false eyelashes to the outer half of
the eye.

4 Finish the look with a slick of lipstick.

TIP: Add adhesive along the length of the false eyelashes and set
aside for a minute until tacky. This will ensure that they quickly
set once applied to the eye.

YOU WILL NEED

liquid foundation
rose-pink blusher
eye shadow in soft taupe
black fine-tip liquid eyeliner
black mascara
2 half-strips of false eyelashes
   and eyelash adhesive
bright red lipstick

PRETTY
in PINK

THIS WILL MAKE EVERY COMPLEXION GLOW.
The shimmering make-up lifts the skin,
whilst the fresh, gentle pink tones will
bring out your features.

1 Evenly apply the liquid foundation to your entire face and dust
with a little powder to take off any shine.

2 To create the eye make-up; brush the soft brown in the eye
socket and blend the cream on top, with the ivory just under the
brow. Use the pale pink over the eyelid. Softly line with a little of
the dark brown along the eyelash line. Apply some mascara and
attach individual lashes to the outer corners of the eyes using a
pair of tweezers.

3 Softly brush a little blusher from the apples of your cheeks
towards your hairline and just below the cheekbone. Gently dot a
little highlighter around the top of the apples of your cheeks and
along the top of your cheekbone and blend with the top edge of
the blusher.

4 Apply the lipstick using a brush, and then add a slick of lip-
gloss to soften.

YOU WILL NEED

liquid foundation
powder foundation
shimmer eye shadow in dark
    brown, soft brown, pale pink,
    cream and ivory
black mascara
individual false eyelashes
    and eyelash adhesive
pink blusher
shimmer highlighter
hot pink lipstick
clear shimmer lip-gloss

1

2

3

4

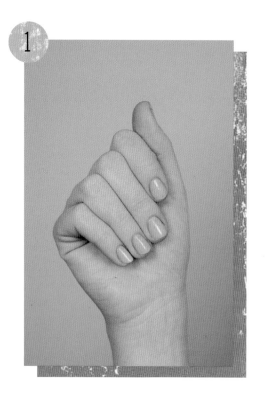

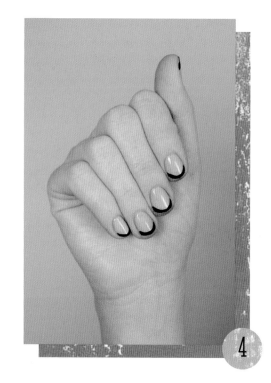

Blue
FRENCH
NAILS

THIS DESIGNER LOOK IS A NEW TAKE ON THE CLASSIC FRENCH MANICURE. This is equally as chic, but far more En Vogue darling!

1 File the nails evenly and add a base coat of clear varnish. Once dry, paint with two coats of nude varnish for an even finish.

2 Use a paintbrush to very carefully paint a thin blue line at the tips of the nails.

3 If you make a mistake you can use the other paintbrush dipped in nail varnish remover as an eraser.

4 Finish with a coat of clear polish for longer wear.

YOU WILL NEED

nail file
clear nail varnish
nude nail varnish
2 fine-art paintbrushes
dark blue nail varnish
nail varnish remover

BEAUTIFUL
BLOSSOM NAILS

THIS GORGEOUS DESIGN LOOKS ELEGANT WITH A FLOATY SUMMERY DRESS. Try using different background shades to match your outfit.

1 Evenly file your nails and add a base coat of clear varnish.

2 Randomly paint the nails using the pastel shades, applying a couple of coats on each.

3 Using the paintbrush, paint on the flowers. These are five small lines fanning out from a central point. Add them as you wish, either one or two per nail.

4 Clean the brush in the nail varnish remover and paint on the stems. Paint a small line running from each flower, if there is more than one flower on a nail then the stems should join. Clean the brush again and add a small dot to the centre of each flower.

YOU WILL NEED

nail file
clear nail varnish
2 complimentary pastel shades of
    nail varnish, i.e. yellow and green
fine-art paintbrush
nail varnish for the flowers, i.e. red
nail varnish remover
nail varnish for the stems,
    i.e. dark brown
nail varnish for the flower centres,
    i.e. light yellow

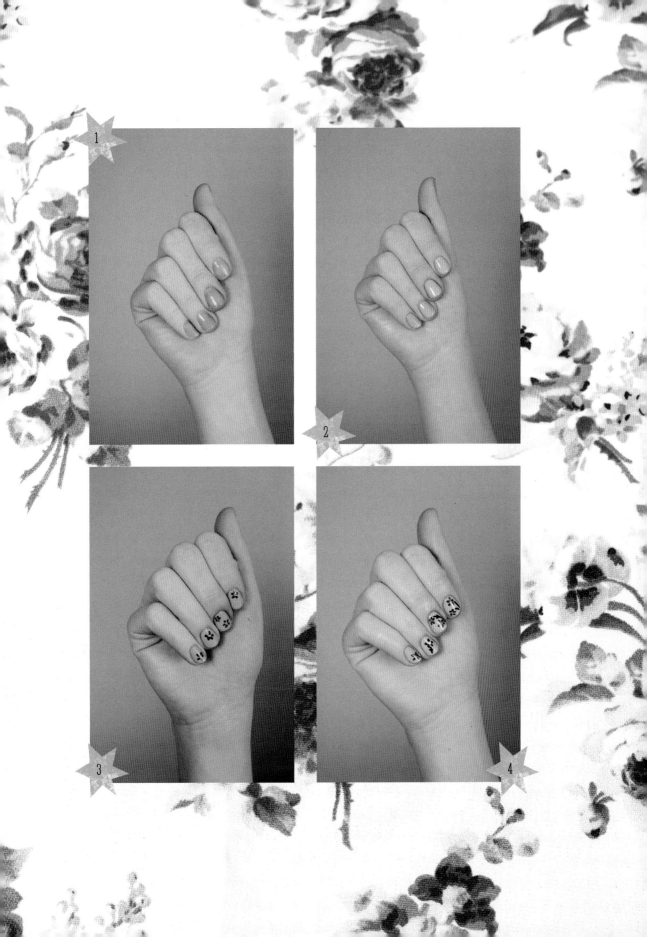

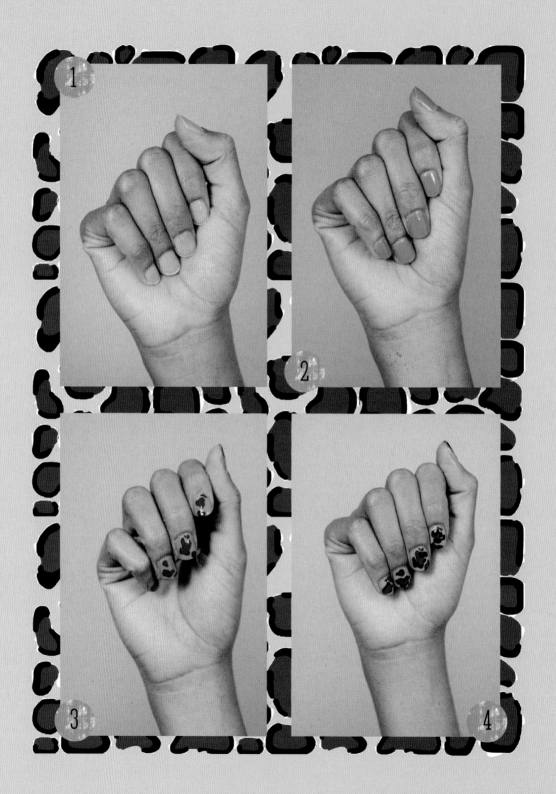

Neo-Leopard
PRINT NAILS

BRIGHTEN YOUR HANDS WITH THIS SUPER
COOL LOOK! Stand out from the crowd
with bold and bright clashing colours.

1 Evenly file your nails and add a base coat of clear varnish.

2 Paint your nails with two coats of background colour.

3 Use a paintbrush to paint the inner leopard pattern in random patches, one large and one small area on each nail. Leave to dry.

4 Clean the brush with nail varnish remover and paint on the outer leopard pattern. Wiggle the brush around edges of the inner patches to get a random animal print feel. Leave to dry. Finish with a coat of clear polish for longer wear.

LAVENDER SALT
HAND SCRUB

200g Epsom salts or coarse sea salt
100ml olive or almond oil
20 drops of lavender essential oil
2–3 tbsp Vitamin E oil (optional)
1–2 tbsp dried lavender flowers (optional)

Mix all the ingredients together in a large bowl. Work a handful of the scrub into your hands and rinse with warm water.

BEFORE A MANICURE OR AFTER A CRAFTING SESSION THERE'S NOTHING LIKE A GOOD EXFOLIATION. The salt purifies, while the oil ensures the skin doesn't dry out. Store the extra in a sterilised airtight container, for example an old jam jar.

HOW TO
Give a
HAND
MASSAGE

IT IS TRULY BLISSFUL WHEN TIRED HANDS ARE MASSAGED. You can either use these techniques for a self-massage or you can treat one of your guests to a lovely, relaxing massage.

Place a towel on your lap. Working with one hand at a time, rub with hand moisturiser or massage oil. Gently massage all the way up to the elbow until the moisturiser has been completely blended into the skin.

Work up from the muscles in the wrists to the elbow using a gentle rotating, squeezing motion. If you are massaging someone else, use both hands to squeeze either side of the arm, working your way up to the elbow. Repeat this action back down.

Turn the hand over and firmly massage the palm and the spaces in between the fingers. Turn the hand over and repeat. Massage each finger individually from top to bottom, then give a gentle twist in both directions and a quick pull to finish.

Slide your hand downwards from the elbow to the fingers, then repeat the process with the other hand.

Mocha
FACE MASK

YOU WILL NEED

4 tbsp finely ground espresso coffee beans
4 tbsp cocoa powder
8 tbsp plain yoghurt

FOR DRY SKIN
2 tbsp honey

FOR OILY SKIN
2 tbsp lemon juice

FOR COMBINATION SKIN
ı tbsp honey
ı tbsp lemon juice

Place all the ingredients in a food blender and blitz until smooth. Apply to your face and neck, taking care to avoid the eye area. Leave on for 10 minutes. Remove using warm water.

CAFFEINE EFFECTIVELY KICK-STARTS YOUR SKIN
- it will decrease puffiness and brighten dull complexions. This is great before a night out, or even the morning after... Keep any extra in a jar in the fridge.

MAKES 4
MASKS

AVOCADO AND BANANA
FACE MASK

YOU WILL NEED

¼ ripe avocado, peeled and mashed
½ ripe banana, peeled and mashed
2 tbsp sour cream
I tsp wheat-germ oil

Place all the ingredients in a food blender and blitz until smooth. Apply to your face and neck, taking care to avoid the eye area. Leave on for 15 minutes. Remove with warm water.

THIS RICH MASK IS IDEAL FOR THOSE WITH DRY TO NORMAL SKIN. IT IS FULL OF PROTEIN, WHICH IS EASILY ABSORBED BY THE SKIN AND WILL HELP PROTECT IT FROM THE ELEMENTS. As it is best when fresh, make this mask just before you want to use it. This is the perfect mask to use before you want to apply make-up.

HOW TO
Give an
EXPRESS
FACIAL

A GOOD FACIAL TREATMENT CAN IMPROVE THE CIRCULATION OF YOUR SKIN, GIVING A REJUVENATING EFFECT. Either use this technique on yourself in front of a mirror or indulge a friend.

Tie back long hair and wrap a towel around your head to keep your hair away from your face.

Remove all make-up and use a facial exfoliator to cleanse the skin. Make small circular motions using the tips of your fingers, working from the chin up towards the hairline. Concentrate on the areas around the nose and forehead. Rinse the skin well.

Fill a bowl with boiling water and place your head over it. Cover the back of your head with a towel to keep in the heat. Steam for 5 minutes, this will open the pores and help remove impurities.

Apply the face mask above or the one on page 101 and follow the instructions. Rinse well. Finish with a good moisturiser.

Lemon and Vodka
FOOT SOAK

YOU WILL NEED

1 egg, lightly beaten
240ml whole milk
120ml lemon juice
100ml vodka
foot cream

Pour the egg, milk, lemon juice and vodka directly into a bowl that is large enough to fit both of your feet and mix well.

Soak your feet for 15 minutes, massaging your toes and ankles while they soak. Towel dry your feet and return them to the bowl to soak for a further 15 minutes.

Rinse your feet with warm water, towel dry and pour the soak away. Finish by rubbing in some foot cream.

OFTEN, OUR FEET ARE NEGLECTED AND IN NEED OF A BIT OF LOVE. This zesty foot soak is a great way to soften skin and soak up moisture. The shot of vodka gives it an antiseptic bonus!

BROWN SUGAR
FOOT SCRUB

YOU WILL NEED

2 tbsp ground oats
2 tbsp brown sugar
2 tbsp Aloe Vera gel
1 tbsp honey
1 tsp fresh lemon juice
1 tsp almond or olive oil

In a food blender, grind the oats until the consistency of coarse sand. Transfer to a large bowl with the remaining ingredients and mix together to form a paste.

Massage into your feet, focusing on dry areas such as your heels and big toes. Rinse well with warm water.

I WANT SOME BROWN SUGAR! This is a great way to exfoliate all the unwanted dead skin from your feet, leaving them feeling smooth and smelling delicious.

Savvy Savouries, Sweet Treats & Cocktails!

Girls' love party food, it's a scientific fact! Here I have collated some fun ideas that are simple to make but have a real wow factor. In the Savvy Savouries section there are some delicious classic sharing recipes including the Rustic Pizza as well as scrumptious designer nibbles like Posh Chorizo Scotch Eggs. The Sweet Treats are always my favourite element to any party so I have created some show-stopping cakes and desserts, such as the Leggy Ruffle Cake and quirky Cupcake in A Cone. To get you in the party mood, don't forget the cocktails. You better make sure there is enough of everything, because it will all be gone before you know it!

RUSTIC
PIZZA
WITH CRUNCHY COLESLAW

MAKES 2
PIZZAS, FOR
4-6 PEOPLE.

YOU WILL NEED

FOR THE PIZZA BASE
250–350ml lukewarm water
1 tbsp active dried yeast
2 tsp clear, runny honey
2 tbsp extra virgin olive oil, plus extra
    for greasing
550g 'OO' premium strong white flour,
    plus extra for dusting
1 tsp salt
½ tsp ground black pepper

FOR THE TOMATO SAUCE
2 tbsp olive oil
1 onion, finely chopped
2 garlic cloves, crushed
1 bay leaf
1 tsp dried oregano
400g can of chopped tomatoes
2 tbsp tomato purée
sea salt and black pepper

FOR THE TOPPING
Use anything you like, but my favourite
toppings include: ham, salami, chorizo,
pancetta, smoked chicken, anchovies,
sundried tomatoes, red onion, olives,
sweetcorn, grilled peppers, chestnut
mushrooms, buffalo mozzarella, basil
and Parmigiano-Reggiano.

To make the pizza base, pour 150ml of the lukewarm water into a bowl and stir in the yeast. Cover with a tea towel and leave in a warm place for 5 minutes. Once rested, add the honey and olive oil and mix until well combined.

Sift the flour and seasoning into a large bowl and make a well in the centre. Pour in the yeast mixture and, using your fingertips, mix together. Gradually add in the remaining water, but stop adding as soon as you have a slightly sticky dough.

Transfer to a lightly floured work surface and kneed for 10 minutes until pliable – it is important that you don't cut corners with this, just think, you are giving your arms a nice workout!

Lightly oil a bowl twice the size of your dough. Transfer the dough to the bowl and cover with a damp tea towel. Leave in a warm place for 1 hour or until the dough has doubled in size.

Meanwhile, make the sauce. Heat the oil in a saucepan, add the onion and fry for 2–3 minutes or until brown. Add the garlic, bay leaf and oregano and cook for 2–3 minutes to release the flavour.

Add the tomatoes and purée. Bring to a boil then lower to a simmer for 15–20 minutes or until it has reduced and thickened. Add seasoning to taste and set aside to cool.

Preheat the oven to 220°C/425°F/gas mark 7.

Once the dough has risen, use your fists to remove air bubbles. Place on a floured work surface and knead until smooth. Split the dough into two.

To shape, flatten one piece of dough into a round using your palms. Then (here comes the fun part) lift it up and slam it down as hard as you can onto the work surface. Using a rolling pin, roll the round until it is as large as your baking tray or pizza tin. Repeat with the other piece of dough.

Cover your baking trays with baking paper and transfer over your bases. Add a generous dollop of sauce and your desired toppings. Bake for 10–15 minutes, or until brown at the edges.

Crunchy Coleslaw

YOU WILL NEED

½ a small white cabbage, thinly sliced
½ a small red cabbage, thinly sliced
1 small white onion, thinly sliced
3 carrots, grated
2 tbsp of full-fat mayonnaise
1 tbsp of sugar
olive oil
sea salt and black pepper

Mix together the chopped vegetables, mayonnaise and sugar. Drizzle with a little olive oil and season to taste with salt and pepper.

NOT MANY NIGHTS IN ARE COMPLETE WITHOUT A PIZZA.

I can honestly and whole-heartedly recommend this recipe as it works every time. The base can be made in advance and decorated later with your desired toppings. I believe that pizza should always be eaten with coleslaw, for me it is just not the same without that extra crunch.

Borough Market
MINI-BURGERS AND CHIPS

YOU WILL NEED

FOR THE BUNS
white bread mix
a little milk, for glazing
sesame seeds

FOR THE BURGERS
1kg lean minced beef
1 small onion, finely chopped
4 tbsp fine breadcrumbs
1 egg, lightly beaten
1 red chilli, finely chopped
1 tsp salt
1 tsp mustard power
½ tsp black pepper
2 garlic cloves, crushed
olive oil, for frying

FOR THE ASSEMBLY
6 tomatoes, sliced
1 small cos lettuce
gherkins, relish and ketchup (optional)

FOR THE CHIPS
6 extra-large floury potatoes, such as
  Maris Piper or King Edward, peeled
200ml vegetable oil
fine sea salt

LIVING IN LONDON I OFTEN MAKE TIME TO VISIT THE WORLD FAMOUS BOROUGH MARKET IN NEARBY LONDON BRIDGE. Taking inspiration from this amazing market, these delicious bite-sized burgers are simply delicious, and the three-way cooked chips are truly divine.

Make the buns first. Follow the bread mix instructions. Cover two baking trays with baking paper. Take a small handful of dough and roll in the palm of your hands to create 2.5cm rounds. You want to make about 20. Spread out on the baking trays. These may look small but they will double in size once left to rise. Cover with a damp tea towel and leave in a warm place for about an hour. Preheat the oven to 220°C/425°F/gas mark 7.

Once risen, brush with milk and sprinkle with sesame seeds. Bake for 15–20 minutes or until golden brown. Leave to cool on a wire rack. These can be stored in a clean, dry box for up to 4 days or kept frozen for up to 3 months.

Make the burgers. Place all the ingredients except the oil in a bowl. Combine together by hand, being careful not to overwork. With wet hands, shape the mixture into 4.5–5cm rounds. They need to be about 1cm-thick and the edges should be smooth.

Heat the oil in a non-stick pan and fry the burgers for 2–3 minutes on each side or until brown. Cook these in batches.

Slice the buns in half and add a slice of tomato, a lettuce leaf and a gherkin, relish and tomato ketchup. Spear the middle of the burger with a toothpick to help it keep its shape.

Make the chips. Slice the potatoes into even sticks, around 7cm long and 1cm thick. Preheat the oven to 200°C/400°F/gas mark 6.

Place the chips in a pan of boiling water and blanch for 3–4 minutes. Strain and pat dry with some kitchen paper.

In a shallow pan or deep fat fryer, bring the oil to a medium heat (about 120°C). Fry the chips a handful at a time for 5–6 minutes – cooking in batches ensures that the oil doesn't loose too much heat. Carefully remove from the oil using a slotted spoon and place on some kitchen paper to remove any excess oil.

Line a baking tray with parchment paper. Bake the chips for 8–10 minutes or until golden brown and crisp on the outside.

To make chip cups, cut 10 x 21cm rectangles from patterned card and roll into funnel shapes. Secure with a dot of glue or a staple.

CHICKEN SATAY
WITH PEANUT DIP

MAKES 16

YOU WILL NEED

4 skinless chicken breast fillets, about 500g,
  cut into quarters

FOR THE MARINADE
1 tbsp clear, runny honey
1 tbsp soy sauce
a few drops of Tabasco sauce
1 garlic clove, crushed
1 tbsp grated fresh ginger

FOR THE PEANUT DIP
1½ tbsp groundnut oil
3 shallots, finely chopped
1 red chilli, seeds discarded and chopped
1 tbsp grated fresh ginger
2 garlic cloves, crushed
100g unsalted, natural roasted peanuts
juice of 1 lime
1½ tbsp soy sauce
1 tbsp light brown sugar
1 tbsp chopped coriander leaves

Mix all the marinade ingredients in a large bowl until combined. Add the chicken and cover with cling film. Leave for at least 30 minutes, but preferably in the fridge overnight.

Soak 16 bamboo skewers in warm water for 20–30 minutes.

Make the dip. Heat the oil in a frying pan and fry the shallots for 2–3 minutes or until soft. Stir in the chilli, ginger and garlic and cook for 2 minutes. Add the peanuts and cook for a further 2 minutes. Remove the pan from the heat and leave to cool.

Place the dip mixture in a food blender with the remaining ingredients. Blitz in quick sharp bursts until a rough consistency.

Preheat the grill to its highest setting. Thread each strip of chicken onto individual skewers. Grill for about 3–4 minutes on each side, or until just cooked. Serve with the dipping sauce.

THIS DISH IS ALWAYS A HIT.
For ease, marinate the chicken the night before.

Posh CHORIZO SCOTCH EGGS

YOU WILL NEED

12 quail's eggs
150g plain flour, plus extra for dusting
300g pork sausage meat (about 4 sausages)
200g chorizo cooking sausage, skin removed and meat roughly blended in a food processor
handful of flat-leaf parsley, finely chopped
1 tsp paprika
sea salt and black pepper
2 large eggs, beaten
110g dried breadcrumbs
vegetable oil, for frying

Boil water in a pan, add the quail's eggs and boil for 4 minutes. Drain and cover with cold water.

Peel the eggs – the best way to crack the shell is to gently roll the eggs on the worktop, then peel them under lukewarm running water. Dry with kitchen paper and dust with a little flour.

In a bowl, mix together the sausage meats, the parsley, paprika and some seasoning.

Lay out a piece of cling film on a flat surface and place a small handful of the meat mixture in the centre. Flatten into a 7–8cm round and place the boiled egg in the middle. Use the cling film to bring the meat mixture up and around the egg until completely enclosed. Repeat with the remaining eggs.

Place the beaten eggs, flour and breadcrumbs in three separate shallow bowls. Dip each meat wrapped egg into the flour, then the egg and finally the breadcrumbs until well covered.

Shallow fry in hot oil for about 5–6 minutes, turn occasionally to brown all over. It is best to cook these in batches. Drain on kitchen paper and eat hot or cold. These can be reheated in the oven at 200°C/400°F/gas mark 6 for 5 minutes.

I MUST ADMIT IT IS ONLY IN RECENT YEARS I HAVE CHANGED MY MIND ABOUT SCOTCH EGGS. Previously I would never have helped myself to them at a party. However, this was before I had tried a chorizo Scotch egg, more of a 'Spanish Egg', the Scotch's far more flamboyant and tasty cousin (hehe).

Bacon & Maple Syrup

1 tsp olive oil
400g thick-cut bacon
50g plain cooked popcorn
180ml maple syrup
½ tsp salt
1 tsp ground black pepper

In a frying pan, heat the oil. Add the bacon, fry until crisp and place on some kitchen paper to remove any excess oil. Reserve 2 tablespoons of the bacon fat from the pan.

Preheat the oven to 170°C/325°F/gas mark 3.

Crumble the bacon and stir into the popcorn along with the reserved fat, syrup, salt and pepper.

Line a baking tray with baking paper and spread the mixture out in a single layer. Bake for 10 minutes, stirring occasionally. Serve hot.

There is no more of a moreish blend than sweet maple syrup and salty bacon. You had better make bucketloads of this, as it will all be gone before you can say supercalifragalistic!

Be transported to Mexico in a mouthful; this amalgamation of flavour brings an authentic che and spice sensation.

MEXICAN

50g plain cooked popcorn
8 tsp grated cheddar cheese
6 tsp grated lime zest
  (about 6 limes)
¼ tsp chilli powder
¼ tsp cayenne pepper
¾ tsp salt
3 tbsp butter, melted

In a large bowl, toss together all the ingredients until combined.

SAVOURY POPCORN

NO MOVIE NIGHT IS COMPLETE WITHOUT
SOME POPCORN, *but we can all get a bit bored
of the same old sweet and salted varieties.
Spice up your options with this surprisingly
good selection of unusual alternatives!*

Citrusy Chilli-Chocolate

50g plain cooked popcorn
4½ tbsp grated dark chocolate
1½ tsp cinnamon
1½ tsp grated orange zest
  (about 1 large orange)
1½ tsp sugar
¼ tsp cayenne pepper
¼ tsp salt
3 tbsp butter, melted

In a large bowl, toss together all
the ingredients until combined.

*This combination
is spicy, sweet and
zesty all at the same time
– it's quite literally
a taste explosion.*

SPICY VEGETABLE
Samosas

MAKES 24

YOU WILL NEED

FOR THE PASTRY
225g plain flour, plus extra for dusting
2 tsp salt
2 tbsp vegetable oil
80ml warm water
vegetable oil, for frying

FOR THE VEGETABLE FILLING
1 tbsp vegetable oil
1 white onion, finely chopped
2 garlic cloves, crushed
2 tbsp curry powder
½ tsp chilli powder
1 large potato, finely diced
1 carrot, finely diced
150g frozen peas
100ml vegetable stock
sea salt and black pepper

AS I AM MARRIED TO AN ANGLO-INDIAN, THERE IS A CONSTANT SMELL OF INDIAN SPICES FROM MY KITCHEN. This recipe comes from my husband's aunt who, like most of his family, is an excellent cook. Use shop-bought filo pastry to reduce cooking time.

To make the pastry, sieve the flour and salt into a large bowl and make a well in the centre. Pour in the oil and gradually add enough water to make a firm, non-sticky dough.

On a floured work surface kneed the dough until smooth. Return to the bowl and cover with cling film. Leave at room temperature for 30 minutes.

Meanwhile make the filling. Heat the oil in a frying pan. Add the onion, garlic, curry and chilli powder and fry for 3–4 minutes or until the onion has become soft. Add the potato, carrot and peas and stir until well combined. Add the stock and a little seasoning, cover and leave to simmer for 30 minutes or until cooked. Leave to cool completely.

Divide the pastry dough into 24 equal pieces. Using wet hands, roll each piece into a ball and use a rolling pin to flatten into a circle about 15cm wide.

Spoon a tablespoon of the cooled filling into one quarter of the circle and dampen the exposed edges with water. Fold the pastry in half over the mixture, creating a semi-circle. Fold the pastry in half again to make into quarters and the typical samosa shape. Repeat with the remaining pastry dough and filling.

Using a deep fat fryer or a deep pan of hot oil (it needs to be deep enough for the samosas to be fully immersed) deep fry the samosas for 3–4 minutes or until crisp and brown. Carefully remove from the oil using a slotted spoon and place on kitchen paper to drain away any excess oil.

POMEGRANATE AND MINT RAITA

Gently mix together 4 tbsp of Greek yoghurt with ½ tsp coriander powder, ½ tsp cumin powder, a handful of chopped mint leaves, a little sea salt and the juice and seeds of half a pomegranate.

Decorate with some extra pomegranate seeds and mint leaves if desired. Chill in the fridge for 10 minutes before serving.

Dorset FISHCAKES
WITH AIOLI

YOU WILL NEED

FOR THE FISHCAKES
300g cold mashed potatoes
6 spring onions, trimmed and thinly sliced
I tbsp horseradish sauce
250g peppered smoked mackerel fillets,
   skin discarded
2 tbsp plain flour
I egg, beaten
85g dried breadcrumbs
sunflower oil, for frying

FOR THE AIOLI
150g mayonnaise
I garlic clove, crushed
sea salt and black pepper
I tsp Dijon mustard
2 tbsp olive oil

In a large bowl, mix together the potato, spring onions and horseradish sauce. Gently flake the mackerel and stir into the potato, trying not to break it up too much.

Using your hands, shape the mixture into about 20 even rounds about 4–5cm in diameter. Slightly flatten and roll in flour to coat. Dip in the egg and cover with the breadcrumbs. Cover and chill until ready to cook.

Gently grill or shallow-fry the fishcakes for 5–6 minutes on each side until crunchy, golden brown and hot all the way through.

To make the aioli, simply mix all the ingredients together in a small bowl. Serve with the hot fishcakes.

MY FAMILY HAVE A HOUSE IN DORSET AND EVERY SUMMER WE HEAD TO THE BEACH AND GO MACKEREL FISHING. There really is nothing more delicious than eating fish straight from the sea; no wonder so many famous chefs come from this area. I love a good fishcake, so here is my bite-size version, which can be prepared a day ahead and kept in the fridge, or pre-cooked and frozen until needed.

MAKES 20

DIPS for CHIPS!

GUACAMOLE

*This classic Mexican dip can be as spicy as you like!
Delicious with tortilla chips. Serve immedietly, or cover
with lemon juice and cling film and keep in the fridge.*

YOU WILL NEED

2 large, ripe avocados, peeled and stoned
½ red onion
1–2 red chillies, seeds removed
2 tbsp chopped coriander leaves
1 tbsp of fresh lime or lemon juice
sea salt and black pepper
1 tomato, seeds and pulp removed and roughly chopped

In a food processor, blitz all the ingredients together
until roughly chopped and some texture still remains.
Transfer to a small bowl.

TZATZIKI

*This traditional Mezze dip is my favourite; it goes really
well with sliced carrots, cucumber or celery sticks.*

YOU WILL NEED

1 small cucumber, peeled and seeds removed
350ml Greek yoghurt
2 tbsp fresh lemon juice
2 garlic cloves, crushed
olive oil, for dressing
paprika, for dressing

Grate the cucumber and, using a clean tea towel,
squeeze out any excess liquid. Transfer to a small
bowl and mix in the yoghurt, lemon juice and garlic.
Drizzle with olive oil and sprinkle over some paprika.

Hummus

*This remains a popular Middle Eastern export. Its
creamy flavour goes perfectly with grilled pitta bread.*

YOU WILL NEED

200g tinned chickpeas, drained and rinsed
2 garlic cloves, crushed
1 tsp ground cumin
100ml tahini paste
4 tbsp water
2 tbsp fresh lemon juice
salt, to taste
olive oil, for dressing
paprika, for dressing

Using a food processor, blend together all of the
ingredients until slightly chunky; add extra salt or
lemon juice to taste. Serve in a low bowl, drizzled
with some olive oil and a sprinkling of paprika.

THESE RECIPES ARE REALLY
USEFUL TO HAVE UP YOUR
SLEEVE, AND EXTRA TASTY
WHEN FRESHLY MADE. The
classic dips always go down
a treat when paired with
crisps, sliced vegetables, pitta
bread and grilled tortillas.
Simple and effective!

Spinach and Ricotta
MINI QUICHES

FOR THE FILLING
1 tbsp olive oil
1 white onion, finely sliced
3 garlic cloves, crushed
200g fresh spinach, washed
4 large eggs, lightly whisked
200g ricotta cheese
100ml single cream
100g cheddar cheese, grated
1 tsp ground cinnamon
sea salt and black pepper

FOR THE PASTRY
butter, for greasing
500g packet of puff pastry
plain flour, for dusting

Preheat the oven to 180°C/350°F/gas mark 4.

Heat the olive oil in a frying pan. Fry the onion and garlic for 2–3 minutes or until lightly browned. Remove from the heat.

Place the spinach in a pan and cook of 2–3 minutes or microwave for 1–2 minutes until it has wilted. Gently squeeze the spinach to remove the excess water and set aside to cool.

In a large bowl mix together all of the remaining and cooled filling ingredients and season to taste.

Butter a 12-hole muffin tin. Roll the pastry out on a floured work surface and cut into 12 equal-sized pieces. Place each piece in a hole of the muffin tin, pat down and cut away any excess from the top. Spoon the mixture into the cases – the mixture will puff up as it cooks so only fill to about two-thirds full.

Bake for 20–25 minutes or until the mixture has hardened and become golden. The filling will sink a little as it cools.

MAKES 12

THESE ARE A TASTY ACCOMPANIMENT
AT ANY PARTY AND ARE PERFECT
FOR YOUR VEGETARIAN GUESTS.
The unusual addition of cinnamon
delightfully compliments both the
cheese and spinach.

BAKED BRIE BARREL
WITH HONEY AND CARAMELISED NUTS

SERVES 8–10

Preheat the oven to 200°C/400°F/gas mark 6.

Place a 250g round of brie in an ovenproof dish. Slice the top, drizzle with olive oil and cover with 2 sprigs of thyme.

Cover with foil and bake for 10–15 minutes, or until the cheese feels soft when pressed.

In a frying pan, melt 1 tbsp of butter and stir in 2 tbsp of light brown sugar and 1 tsp of cinnamon. Add a handful each of walnuts and pecans and caramelise the nuts by tossing them in the sugar for about 2 minutes. Remove from the heat.

Drizzle the baked brie with 2 tbsp of clear, runny honey and sprinkle the spiced nuts over the top. Serve with slices of toasted French bread.

Peaches and Cream
LEGGY RUFFLE CAKE

YOU WILL NEED

FOR THE SPONGE
310g self-raising flour
85g ground almonds
225g butter, softened
400g caster sugar
4 eggs
1½ tsp almond extract
1½ tsp vanilla extract
250ml milk

FOR THE FILLING
300ml whipping cream
225g of fresh raspberries
1 tin of peach slices, drained

FOR THE RUFFLE FROSTING
75g butter, at room temperature
550g icing sugar, sieved
1½ tbsp vanilla extract
4 tbsp milk
pink food colouring

104 Wilton decorating tip, or similar
   petal-shaped nozzle
piping bag
palette knife

SERVES 8-10

Preheat the oven to 180°C/350°F/gas mark 4. Line three 20cm cake tins. You may need to bake these in batches.

Sieve the flour and almonds into a mixing bowl and set aside.

In a large bowl, cream together the butter and sugar until light and fluffy. Beat the eggs in one at a time, adding a tablespoon of flour if the mixture starts to curdle. Stir in both extracts.

Beat in a third of the flour then a third of the milk, and repeat until both are incorporated. Pour into the prepared tins. Bake for 25–30 minutes or until a skewer inserted into the centre of the cake comes out clean. Cool on a wire rack.

Make the filling. Using an electric whisk on a medium-fast setting, whip the cream in a large bowl until it becomes stiff.

Place a sheet of baking paper on a rotating cake stand or flat plate. Place the first cake on the stand and cover the top with half the cream. Lay half the raspberries and peaches on top of the cream. Place the second cake on top and repeat the cream and fruit filling. Cover with the third cake.

For the frosting, whisk together the butter and icing sugar. Beat in the vanilla, milk and a few drops of food colouring – you want to create a pastel pink colour.

Spoon half of the frosting onto the top of the cake and using a palette knife, spread evenly and thinly over the top and sides. This doesn't have to be perfect as it will be hidden by the ruffles.

Attach the petal nozzle to the bag and fill with frosting. With the thinner point of the nozzle facing upwards, ice an overlapping 2cm-wide zigzag from the top of the cake to the bottom, working in as straight a line as possible. Once you have reached the bottom, start a new line back up at the top, overlapping the first line. Repeat until the sides are completely covered. You now need to ice the top. Starting at the central point, repeat the zigzag motion, getting bigger as you work outwards. It should look as if you have iced each slice at a time.

To make the leggy topper, transfer the template on page 184 onto thin card and cut out. Stick two toothpicks to the back and insert in the middle of the cake.

THIS CAKE TRULY IS THE
ULTIMATE SHOWSTOPPER,
guaranteed to put a smile
on all your guest's faces.
Its got layers of pink frills
in delicious vanilla frosting,
moreish almond sponge
filled with delectable
peaches, raspberries and
cream, all topped off with
a great pair of legs… what
more could a girl want?!

Banoffee
ICE-CREAM CAKE

YOU WILL NEED

FOR THE CAKE
4 bananas, sliced into 1cm rounds
200g digestive biscuits
50g butter, melted
2 egg whites
450g good-quality vanilla ice-cream
10g white chocolate, grated (optional)

FOR THE TOFFEE
85g butter
210g light brown sugar
150ml heavy cream

THIS IS A MODERN TWIST ON THE EVER
POPULAR BANOFFEE PIE. The soft
layers of ice-cream paired with
the delectable caramel and biscuit
base makes this cake a triumph.
As this recipe is done in stages
it's a great one to do as you are
getting other things ready.

Place the sliced bananas in a metal bowl and keep in the freezer for 1–2 hours.

Meanwhile, place the biscuits in a re-sealable food bag and bash with a rolling pin until fine crumbs. Transfer to a mixing bowl and stir in the melted butter. Line the bottom of a 18cm round springform tin with some baking parchment. Spoon in the biscuit mixture and pat down until firm and level.

Place the bananas in a blender, add the egg whites and blitz until it is a smooth mixture with no lumps. The egg whites will stop the mixture from becoming too hard. Spoon the mixture on top of the biscuit base – the tin should be about half full (it will be dependent on the size of the bananas). Smooth level and place in the freezer for 30 minutes.

Now make the toffee. In a saucepan, melt the butter over a medium to high heat. Add the sugar and stir vigorously. Take off the heat, count to ten and pour in the cream, stirring vigorously.

When the banana layer feels firm, remove from freezer and pour over half of the toffee mixture. Return to the freezer for a further 15 minutes, but be careful not to let the toffee fully harden.

Spoon the vanilla ice-cream into the mixer and blend to a paste. Place on top of the toffee layer and smooth level. Sprinkle over the chocolate and return to the freezer for at least 1 hour.

Transfer the dish to the fridge 20 minutes before serving to allow the cake to soften slightly. One softened, unclip the side of the tin, remove the baking paper and carefully transfer onto a serving plate. Drizzle over the remaining toffee and serve.

This cake can be kept in the freezer for up to 2 weeks.

A CUPCAKE IN A CONE? WHAT SORT OF
TASTY TRICKERY IS THIS? TRUST ME,
IT IS THE VERY BEST KIND! Yes, this
ingenious invention is not only filled
with chocolaty deliciousness, but
it is practical too; no spillage, no
waste, just gorgeous! ...oh, and very,
very tasty.

Cupcake
IN A CONE

YOU WILL NEED

FOR THE CUPCAKES
12 flat-based ice-cream cones
35g cocoa powder
65ml hot water
110g self-raising flour
½ tsp salt
120g unsalted butter
175g caster sugar
2 eggs, beaten
1 tsp vanilla extract
85ml sour cream

FOR THE FROSTING
300g icing sugar
150g unsalted butter
2 tsp vanilla extract
2½ tbsp single cream

FOR DECORATION
85g dark chocolate, broken
12 Maraschino cherries with stems
   or glacé cherries

Preheat the oven to 180°C/350°F/gas mark 4. Place the ice-cream cones into a 12-hole muffin tin.

In a small bowl, mix together the cocoa powder and hot water until smooth. Sieve the flour and salt into another bowl.

Melt the butter in a small saucepan, transfer to a mixing bowl and whisk with the sugar until cool. Continue to whisk, adding an egg at a time. Add a spoonful of flour if it starts to curdle. Stir in the vanilla and the cocoa mixture. Add the flour a tablespoon at a time, alternating with the sour cream. Mix until smooth.

Spoon the mixture into the cones until half full. Bake in the oven for 20–25 minutes or until springy to the touch and an inserted skewer comes out clean. Place on a wire rack to cool.

To make the frosting, sieve the icing sugar into a large bowl and beat with the butter until smooth. Mix in the vanilla extract and cream until well combined.

Using a dessertspoon, scoop some frosting onto the tops of the cones and use a knife to smooth into ice-cream scoop shapes. Transfer to a plate and place in the fridge for 15 minutes.

Place the chocolate in a heatproof bowl. Set over a saucepan of boiling water, making sure that the bottom of the bowl does not touch the water. Stir until the chocolate is melted and glossy.

Remove the cooled cakes from the fridge and use a teaspoon to drizzle the chocolate over the top of the cakes. The cooling process should ensure that the frosting does not separate. Add a cherry to the top whilst the chocolate is still warm. Repeat with the remaining cakes and return to the fridge until the chocolate is hard to the touch.

PARIS BREST

IMAGINE A RING OF DELICATE PROFITEROLES filled with velvety fresh cream and luxurious vanilla custard, drizzled with dark chocolate and finished with a sprinkling of warm roasted almonds. This isn't just any Brest, this is a Paris Brest…

SERVES
6

Preheat the oven to 210°C/410°F/gas mark 6.

Trace around a 22cm circular plate onto baking paper. Turn the paper over so that the pencil mark is on the underside and lay on top of a baking sheet.

Place the butter and water in a saucepan and bring the mixture to the boil over a medium heat. Sift in the flour. Using a wooden spoon, beat the mixture vigorously for 1–2 minutes or until it comes away from the sides of the pan. Transfer to a mixing bowl and leave to cool for about 5 minutes.

Using an electric whisk, beat the eggs into the mixture one at a time. Fit the round nozzle and fill the piping bag with the dough. Pipe 4–5cm rounds, just touching one another, following along the traced line until you have a wreath shape. Bake for 30–35 minutes or until puffed up and golden. Transfer to a wire rack and allow to cool completely.

Meanwhile, toast the almonds in a dry frying pan over a low heat for 5 minutes until golden and fragrant. Do not let them burn.

In a large bowl, whisk together the cream and icing sugar until thick and fluffy.

Take your time with this next stage. Very carefully cut the pastry ring in half horizontally using a bread or other sharp knife. Lift the top off and place to one side. Fit the star nozzle to another piping bag and pipe a layer of cream onto the base. Spoon a layer of custard on top and replace the top of the pastry ring right side up. Carefully transfer to the fridge for 30 minutes or until chilled.

Place the chocolate in a heatproof bowl over a saucepan filled with simmering water, making sure that the bottom of the bowl does not touch the water. Using a metal spoon, stir the chocolate until it has melted and has become glossy. Use a spoon to drizzle over the pastry, sprinkle with the toasted almonds and serve.

Cupcakes
IN A JAR

WITH STRAWBERRIES
AND CREAM

INSPIRED BY SUMMER DAYS, THIS UBER-FASHIONABLE CAKE IS MADE WITH FRESH STRAWBERRIES AND CREAM. As they are self-contained, they are great for making alongside craft projects that require clean fingers. Why not enjoy with a glass of Champagne or the Wild Hannah cocktail, to experience the full summertime effect!

YOU WILL NEED

200g unsalted butter, plus extra
   for greasing
200g self-raising flour, plus extra
   for dusting
200g caster sugar
4 large eggs, lightly beaten
1 tsp baking powder
2 tsp vanilla extract

FOR THE FILLING
600ml whipping cream
1 tsp vanilla extract
6 tbsp strawberry jam
400g strawberries, stalks removed
   and sliced
coloured sprinkles, for decorating

6 large or 12 small washed jam jars
   (labels removed) or glass tumblers

MAKES
6 LARGE OR
12 SMALL

Preheat the oven to 180°C/350°F/gas mark 4.

For smaller jars you will need a 12-hole cupcake tin and for larger jars a 6-hole muffin tin. Double-check the size of cake you need to make by placing your chosen jar over the holes of the trays – the holes of the tray should be completely covered by the base of your jar. Grease the baking tray and lightly dust with flour.

In a mixing bowl, beat together the butter and sugar until pale and fluffy. Add the egg in two batches, mixing well after each addition. Sift the flour and baking powder into the butter mixture and gently fold to combine. Add the vanilla extract and mix until smooth.

Fill the holes of the baking tray until two-thirds full. Depending on the size, bake for 10–15 minutes or until golden and an inserted skewer comes out clean. Transfer to a wire rack to cool.

Meanwhile make the filling. In a large bowl, using an electric whisk, beat together the cream and vanilla extract until thick and fluffy.

To fill your jars, first cut the cupcakes in half horizontally. Place the bottom half in the jar, add a tablespoon (or half a tablespoon if making 12 small jars) of strawberry jam and a good handful of strawberries. Pipe or spoon a generous layer of the cream to cover and add the top of the cupcake. Using a piping bag fitted with a star nozzle, pipe another layer of cream on top of the cupcake. Decorate with sprinkles and serve.

Pop-tastic!
ICE LOLLIES

THERE IS NOTHING MORE FUN THAN AN ICE LOLLY, and here is a great way to present them. Use any small, intrestingly shaped cake moulds, such as Dariole and Brioche tins.

EQUIPMENT
6 ice-lolly sticks, cut to size
6 small cake tins, 6–10cm tall
Six 10 x 10cm squares of
  extra-strong foil

Mango and Mint Smoothie

A tropical concoction, this fruity lolly goes really well with a splash of white rum.

YOU WILL NEED
250ml light evaporated milk
300g tin of mango slices, drained
handful of mint leaves, chopped
100ml orange juice

In a food blender, blitz the evaporated milk, mango and mint until smooth. Add the orange juice and blitz again.

Pour the mixture into the 6 tins. Place a foil square over each tin and push an ice-lolly stick into the centre of each. Transfer to the freezer for 2 hours, or until completely frozen.

Remove from the freezer 5 minutes before serving. Carefully remove the lollies from the tins. If they prove difficult to remove, briefly place the tin under running water to loosen.

BERRY CHEESECAKE

This has a lovely rich flavour. Add a dash of Crème de Cassis if you want an alcoholic twist.

YOU WILL NEED

200g fresh or frozen mixed summer fruits, e.g.
   strawberries, raspberries, cherries,
   redcurrants and blackcurrants
100g caster sugar
300g light cream cheese

Place the fruit in a saucepan over a high heat and bring to the boil for 4 minutes. Remove from the heat and stir in the sugar until dissolved. Mix in the cream cheese and leave to cool before spooning into the 6 tins.

Position the squares of foil over the top of each tin and push an ice-lolly stick into the centres. Transfer to the freezer for 2 hours, or until completely frozen.

Remove the tins from the freezer 5 minutes before serving and carefully remove the lollies from the tins. If they prove difficult to remove, briefly place the tin under running water to loosen.

MARGARITA

The fresh lime juice gives these a real punch and it is an unusual way to present a cocktail. They also taste great without the alcohol.

YOU WILL NEED

100g caster sugar
200ml fresh lime juice (about 4–5 large limes)
juice of 1 lemon
125ml water
2 tbsp tequila
2 tbsp orange liqueur

Place the sugar, lime juice, lemon juice and water in a small saucepan over a medium heat. Stir until all the sugar has dissolved. Remove from the heat and leave to cool.

Once cool, add the tequila and orange liqueur and whisk until well combined.

Pour the mixture into the 6 tins. Place a foil square over each and push an ice-lolly stick into each centre. Transfer the tins to the freezer for 2 hours, or until completely frozen.

Remove the tins from the freezer 5 minutes before serving and carefully remove the lollies from the tins. If they prove difficult to remove, briefly place the tin under running water to loosen.

ROCKY ROAD
'Slug Cake'

MY MUM CAME UP WITH THIS EXCELLENT BRITISH VERSION OF THE TRADITIONAL AMERICAN ROCKY ROAD AND LIKES TO CALL IT 'SLUG CAKE' because when she was little she thought that the biscuits looked like slugs! My family love this so much that my mum made it as my brothers wedding cake!

In a heavy-based saucepan, melt the butter over a gentle heat. Add the chocolate and golden syrup and stir until smooth. Remove from the heat. Transfer about 125ml of the mixture into a small bowl and set aside.

Fold the biscuit pieces and any crumbs into the remaining chocolate mixture, then stir in the marshmallows and almonds. Scrape the mixture into a 20cm square baking tin and smooth the top with a wet spatula. Pour over the bowl of reserved chocolate mixture and smooth the top level.

Refrigerate for at least 2 hours, but preferably overnight.

When ready to serve, cut into squares using a warmed knife.

YOU WILL NEED

250g unsalted butter

600g best-quality dark chocolate, broken into pieces

6 tbsp golden syrup

400g Nice biscuits, broken into quarters

100g mini marshmallows

120g whole blanched almonds

Sumptuous
CHOCOLATE BLOCK

YOU WILL NEED

9 x 200g bars of best-quality dark, milk and white chocolate (at least 800g needs to be in one type)

SUGGESTED TOPPINGS:
pecans, almonds, candied ginger, cherries, caramel and marshmallows

YOU WILL HAVE SEEN THESE BLOCKS IN EXPENSIVE CHOCOLATE SHOPS, and I think that this has to be one of the most fabulous and simple ideas in the book. However, you must use the best-quality chocolate for it to be absolutely scrumptious.

Break up all of the chocolate and place each type in a separate heatproof bowl. One at a time, place the bowls over a pan of boiling water, making sure that the bottom of the bowl does not touch the water. Stir until smooth and glossy, and repeat with the remaining chocolates. White chocolate can sometimes be too solid in consistency – if this is the case, mix in a little melted butter, this should thin the chocolate and make it the same runny consistency as the other chocolates.

Line a baking tray that has raised sides with baking paper. First pour over the majority chocolate. Taking care as it can get very hot, pour all of the base chocolate onto the baking tray and spread into a large rectangular shape using a palette knife.

Drizzle over the other types of chocolates in swirly, random patterns then sprinkle over your chosen toppings. Leave to cool slightly before you place in the fridge to solidify.

Keep in the fridge until ready to serve. Cut into slices using a warmed knife or serve whole and break up with your hands!

CANDYFLOSS
Cupcakes

YOU WILL NEED

FOR THE CUPCAKES
50g unsalted butter
160g caster sugar
145g plain flour
2 tsp baking powder
½ tsp salt
140ml whole milk
1 egg, lightly whisked
1 tsp vanilla extract

FOR THE FROSTING
350g icing sugar, sieved
120g unsalted butter
30ml whole milk
1 tsp vanilla extract
pink and blue food colouring
selection of coloured candyfloss

1cm star nozzle
piping bag

Preheat your oven to 170°C/325°F/gas mark 3. Line a 12-hole cupcake tin with 12 cases.

Make the cupcakes. In a mixing bowl whisk together the butter and sugar until light and fluffy. Add the flour, baking powder and salt and mix until it is the consistency of fine breadcrumbs. Stir in the milk, egg and vanilla extract and mix until smooth.

Spoon the mixture into the cases until two-thirds full. Bake in the oven for 20–25 minutes or until springy to the touch and a light golden brown. Transfer to a wire rack and leave to cool.

Meanwhile, beat the icing sugar and butter together in a large bowl until pale and fluffy. Stir in the milk and the vanilla.

Separate the frosting into two bowls and mix a few drops of pink food colouring with one and a few drops of blue food colouring to the other. Do not add too much colouring as you want the frosting to be pastel shades.

Fit the piping bag with the nozzle and fill with frosting. Pipe onto the cooled cupcakes. Just before serving, decorate each with small handfuls of candyfloss. Serve immediately as the candyfloss will wilt in a warm room.

BE TRANSPORTED TO A MAGICAL LAND WITH THESE EASY-TO-MAKE CANDYFLOSS CUPCAKES. I was so excited by this recipe, I immediately went out and bought a candyfloss machine! The clouds of fluffy topping go perfectly with the extra-light vanilla sponge.

My Award Winning:

LUXE DARK CHOCOLATE BLACK FOREST GÂTEAU

WITH KIRSCH-SOAKED CHERRIES

Place the cherries in a bowl and pour over enough Kirsch to cover them. Set aside for at least 1 hour or preferably overnight. The longer they soak the tastier they will be.

Preheat the oven to 170°C/325°F/gas mark 3. Grease and line three 20cm round cake tins with baking paper.

Using an electric whisk, beat the butter and sugar until pale and fluffy. Add the eggs one at a time and whisk for 4–5 minutes or until the mixture becomes light. Gently fold in the flour and cocoa powder using a metal spoon.

Spoon equal amounts of the mixture into the three cake tins and level with a palette knife. Bake for 20–25 minutes or until the cakes are springy to the touch and an inserted skewer comes out clean. Allow the cakes to cool in the tins.

Using a cookery brush, paint the tops of the cakes with the Kirsch the cherries are soaking in. Turn the cakes out onto a wire rack and brush the other side with more Kirsch.

To make the icing, heat 250ml of the cream in a pan until just bubbling. Remove from the heat and stir in 100g of the chocolate until melted. Pour into a bowl and place in the fridge to cool.

In a large bowl, whisk the remaining cream until thick and fluffy.

To construct the gâteau, place one of the cakes on a cake stand or turntable. Spoon half of the whipped cream on top and smooth with a knife. Strain the cherries, retaining the alcohol as this can be served alongside the cake as an indulgent drink. Place half the cherries over the cream, covering it. Repeat this process with the next layer, then top with the final cake.

Reserving a heaped tablespoon of the icing for later, cover the whole of the outside of the cake with the rest of the icing. Use a palette knife to smooth the icing over the top and sides.

Melt the remaining 300g of chocolate in a heatproof bowl over a pan of boiling water, making sure it does not touch the water.

YOU WILL NEED

2 x 425g tins of pitted black cherries, drained
500ml bottle of Kirsch or cherry brandy
340g unsalted butter, plus extra for greasing
340g golden caster sugar
6 eggs
240g self-raising flour, sieved
100g cocoa powder, sieved

To create the chocolate leaves, use the brush to paint the front of the bay leaf with the melted chocolate and place chocolate side down on a baking tray. Repeat with the remaining leaves and transfer to the fridge for 10 minutes to harden. Once set, carefully peel away the bay leaves to reveal the chocolate leaves underneath. A good way to do this is to simultaneously peel the bay leaf away from both ends. Dust with some silver to reveal the beautiful veins of the leaves.

Line a baking tray with baking paper. Glue the paper in place on the tray with melted chocolate at each corner.

Measure the height of the cake and use a piece of string to measure the width. Using the brush, paint a rectangle of melted chocolate a bit taller and a bit wider than the cake, about 2–3mm thick. Transfer to the fridge and allow to fully cool and harden. Remove from the fridge and allow to warm up slightly. Using a knife, cut the chocolate into strips that are about 5cm in width.

Carefully peel the strips away from the paper and stick to the sides of the cake using the reserved icing. Wrap with 1cm-wide black ribbon and cut to size leaving a 2cm overlap. Discreetly attach the ends using double-sided tape.

Decorate the cake with the chocolate leaves, mixed fruit and a sprinkling of silver dust.

FOR THE ICING
600ml double cream
400g 85% dark chocolate, broken

FOR THE DECORATION
clean paintbrush
10 bay leaves
edible silver dust or spray
a variety of mixed fruits, e.g. figs,
  raspberries, redcurrants,
  blackcurrants, strawberries,
  or blackberries

SERVES 8

THE FIRST AND ONLY TIME THAT I HAVE ENTERED A BAKING COMPETITION WAS FOR THE BELLENDEN BUN FIGHT, a charity event held in the courtyard of my local bookshop, Review. I must say, being a competitive girl I was disappointed that this beauty only came second, but once you make this for your girls you'll know it's an all-time winner!

Pink Lady

The cocktail synonymous with a cinematic classic,
Grease, in which a group of girls named their gang
'the pink ladies'. Also favoured by the gorgeous Jayne
Mansfield, who was said to have one before every meal.

YOU WILL NEED

44ml gin
1½ tsp lemon juice
1 tsp grenadine syrup
1 tsp single cream
1 egg white
ice-cubes

Place all the ingredients in a cocktail shaker. Shake
vigorously, then strain into a chilled cocktail glass.

WHITE LADY

This Lady has a far subtler and more citrusy flavour
than the others.

YOU WILL NEED

60ml dry gin
15ml Cointreau
15ml lemon juice
1 egg white
ice-cubes

Place all the ingredients in a cocktail shaker.
Shake vigorously, then strain into a chilled
cocktail glass.

BLUE LADY

The strongest of the bunch, it is made with almost 100%
alcohol. Warning – this will turn your tongue blue!

YOU WILL NEED

60ml gin
30ml Blue Curacao
15ml lemon juice
ice-cubes
1 Maraschino cherry

Place the spirits, lemon juice and ice in a cocktail
shaker and shake vigorously. Strain into a chilled
cocktail glass. Make a small incision in the bottom of
the cherry and place on the side of the glass.

MAKES 1
GLASS

CALLING ALL
Ladies

IT SEEMS THAT THERE IS A PLETHORA OF LOVELY 'LADY' COCKTAILS TO CHOOSE FROM. Names range from Foxy to Bearded, Cocaine to Apricot and White to Black, with over seventy variations in between! The queen of these has to be the Pink Lady: a sugary-sweet bubblegum-tasting drink that was popular in the 1930's for being the ultimate 'girly' tipple.

To make the pretty lady drinks toppers, colour photocopy the ladies here onto thin card and cut out. Stick a toothpick to the back and place in your drink.

TO MAKE A FLAG
Cross two bamboo skewers
and tie them together in the middle
using some string. Cut two triangles out of your
chosen fabric – they need to be slightly larger than the
L-shapes created by the crossed skewers. Attach the edges of the
fabric to the bamboo stick using a glue gun and add
some twine for extra nautical decoration.

TITANIC

YOU WILL NEED

ice-cubes
45ml vodka
15ml dry martini
15ml Galliano Italian liqueur
15ml blue Curacao
Indian tonic water (optional)

OH YES, YOU GUESSED IT, THIS IS THE PERFECT ACCOMPANIMENT TO THE MOVIE, although you may be surprised to hear that this drink is not meant to be served on a great heap of ice! It has a bitter-orange and vanilla flavour, which is strangely moreish, a bit like Leo…

Half fill a cocktail shaker with ice cubes and add the rest of the ingredients. Shake vigorously and pour into a short glass. If you want to make this as a punch, top up with tonic water.

'I'M THE KING OF THE WORLD!'

Flora FIZZ

YOU WILL NEED

edible flowers
small-cube ice-cube tray
60ml gin
15ml fresh lemon juice
15ml pink grapefruit juice
22ml elderflower liqueur
a dash of grenadine
60ml champagne

First make the floral ice-cubes. Insert a flower into each section of an ice-cube tray and top with water. Freeze.

Place all the ingredients, except the champagne and ice-cubes, in a cocktail shaker. Shake to mix and then strain into a champagne glass. Top up with the champagne and add the floral ice-cubes.

IF YOU LOVE CHAMPAGNE AND THE AROMA OF DELICATE FLOWERS, you are clearly a super-sophisticated lady who will greatly enjoy sipping this delight. Created for one of my closest friends, Flora – a terribly fitting name for this beautiful creation.

GINGER DRIVER

MAKES 1 GLASS

YOU WILL NEED

ice-cubes
45ml citrus vodka
90ml orange juice
60ml grapefruit juice
ginger ale

Place some ice in a highball glass or clean jam jar.

Pour the vodka and orange and grapefruit juices into a cocktail shaker and stir. Pour over the ice and top with ginger ale.

THIS IS MY VERSION OF THE CLASSIC SCREWDRIVER, topped with some ginger ale for a much zestier flavour. Designed for a close friend who not only is ginger but has the surname Driver… genius!

NOTE: THIS DRINK WILL NOT TURN YOU GINGER!

Boot BLASTER

MAKES 1 GLASS

YOU WILL NEED

ice-cubes
30ml white rum
30ml gin
30ml vodka
30ml triple sec
juice of ½ a lemon
juice of ½ a lime
coca cola
wedges of lemon, to serve

THIS WILL REALLY BLOW YOUR BOOTS OFF – the combination of rum, gin, vodka and triple sec is a recipe for a blaster!

Half fill a glass – preferably one that is shaped like a boot – with ice. Pour the spirits over the ice, then add the lemon and lime juice. Top with a little cola, place a wedge of lemon on the side of the glass and serve.

COSMOPOLITAN

THESE ALCOHOLIC JELLY SHOTS NOT
ONLY LOOK BEAUTIFUL BUT THEY
TASTE MIGHTY FINE TOO!
Serve in pretty foil sweet or
cake cases.

YOU WILL NEED

5 leaves of gelatine
180ml vodka
120ml Cointreau
120ml cranberry juice
juice of 1 lime

2 silicone ice-cube trays
baking sheet
foil sweet cases

MAKES 36
JELLIES

Soak the gelatine leaves in cold water until they become soft. Drain.

Pour the vodka, Cointreau and cranberry and lime juices into a saucepan and heat until warm but not boiling. Stir in the gelatine leaves until they are fully dissolved, then allow the mixture to cool for a few minutes until lukewarm.

Place the ice-cube trays on a baking tray so that they are easy to transport and pour the mixture into the trays. Place in the fridge, preferably overnight, but for at least 2 hours. They are set when they are firm to the touch.

When you are ready to serve, remove from the fridge. Carefully run a very sharp knife around the outside of all the jelly squares to loosen and gently turn them out into foil cases.

Girls' Gossip
MOJITO PUNCH

YOU WILL NEED

5 large limes, quartered

3 tbsp caster sugar

ice-cubes

250g strawberries, plus extra
for serving

a large handful of mint, stems
discarded and leaves crushed

130g light brown sugar

470ml white rum

1 litre soda water

WHEN THE GIRLS GET TOGETHER ALL THEY WANT TO DO IS HAVE A CATCH-UP AND A GOSSIP AND NOTHING GETS THE CONVERSATION FLOWING LIKE A GOOD PUNCH! This heavenly mixture of limes, strawberries, mint, rum and brown sugar will get those chatterboxes well oiled!

Run one of the lime quarters around the rim of each cocktail glass and dip into the caster sugar to create a pretty rim.

Squeeze all the juice from the remaining lime quarters into a punch bowl and add some ice. Quarter the strawberries and discard the stems. Stir in the strawberries, mint and brown sugar.

Mix in the rum and add enough soda water for the sugar to fully dissolve. Ladle into the sugared glasses and serve with a whole strawberry inserted onto the side of each glass.

THE GOSSIP TEST!

SEE IF YOU ARE A LOYAL LADY OR A BIG FAT GOSSIP!
Answer A, B or C to the following questions...

1. If a friend told you a juicy secret, would you:

A. Immediately call another friend to tell them.
B. Sit on it for a while, then gently bring it up
in conversation.
C. Not say a word, your lips are sealed!

2. You overhear a conversation that you really weren't supposed to that involves someone you know, do you:

A. Tell your friends the story, it's their fault for talking
so loud!
B. Tell the person involved what you heard.
C. Pretend it never happened, it is none of
your business.

3. Out of the following which is your favourite magazine?

A. Grazia.
B. Red.
C. Good Housekeeping.

ANSWERS
Mostly A's – Ooh, you big fat gossip! You will take any opportunity to go telling tales on almost anyone. You are bold as brass and are not shy of letting the world know.

Mostly B's – You don't go out of your way to gossip, but if it falls in your lap who are you to stop it! You care about your friends and will defend them no matter what, but you also like a bit of a laugh as much as the next person.

Mostly C's – You are a loyal and kind friend, who takes her responsibilities seriously. You are not afraid to stand up for what you believe in, but generally like a quiet life without too much confrontation.

MAKES 1
GLASS

Cookies and Cream

*Perfect for any chocolate addict, the crushed Oreo
biscuit topping is a serious treat – heaven in a glass!*

YOU WILL NEED
2 Oreo biscuits (about 20g)
60ml whipping cream
60ml single cream
20ml Frangelico or other hazelnut liqueur
20ml Kahlua or other coffee liqueur
20ml Baileys or other Irish cream liqueur
2 tsp clear, runny honey
ice-cubes

Place the biscuits in a sealed sandwich bag and, using
a rolling pin, beat until coarsely crushed.

In a large bowl, whisk the whipping cream until firm
peaks form.

Place the single cream, Frangelico, Kahlua, Baileys,
honey, a handful of ice-cubes and half the broken
biscuits into a blender and blitz until the ice is
crushed and the mixture is well combined.

Pour into a large glass. Top with the whipped cream
and sprinkle with the remaining crushed biscuits.
Serve immediately.

Sweet
SHOP

RHUBARB AND CUSTARD
*This childhood favourite makes a gorgeous half and half
cocktail; the custard Advocaat sits at the bottom of the
glass whilst the rhubarb syrup mixture sits on top.*

YOU WILL NEED
60ml Advocaat liqueur
60ml gin
60ml syrup, drained from tinned rhubarb
ice-cubes
fresh mint leaf, to garnish

Pour the Advocaat into a tall, thin glass.

In a cocktail mixer, shake together the gin, syrup and
ice-cubes. Slowly pour the rhubarb mixture through a
strainer into the glass. Garnish with a mint leaf.

MAKES 1 GLASS

MAKES 1 GLASS

POPCORN MARTINI

This stunning cocktail is made from popcorn syrup combined with flavoured vodka producing an authentic caramel popcorn taste. And the popping candy around the rim of the glass puts the pop back into the popcorn!

YOU WILL NEED

120ml popcorn syrup (see right)
60ml vanilla or butterscotch flavoured vodka
15ml double cream
clear, runny honey
⅓ of a 5g sachet of popping candy
multi-coloured sprinkle decorations

In a cocktail mixer shake together the popcorn syrup, vodka and the cream.

Using your finger, brush the rim of the glass with honey and dip into a bowl containing popping candy and sprinkles. Pour in the drink and serve.

THIS LITTLE COLLECTION IS A FLASHBACK TO MY FAVOURITE CHILDHOOD SWEETS, WITH AN OBVIOUS ADDED KICK! They work great together, so you can offer your party guests a choice of sweetie delights!

POPCORN SYRUP
MAKES ENOUGH FOR 6 GLASSES

Make 200g popcorn by following the packet instructions. Bring 3 pints of water to a boil in a large saucepan. Add 200g caster sugar and 2 tsp salt and stir until dissolved. Stir in the cooked popcorn a handful at a time and simmer for 15 minutes. Use a sieve to strain the liquid into a bowl. You may need to do this in two batches. Shake the popcorn in the sieve but do not push down, then discard. Pour the reserved liquid into a jug and leave to cool at room temperature. Once cool, strain the liquid again and discard any thick residue left in the sieve. Strain again if required. Return the liquid to the jug and place in the fridge until needed.

BEARDED Lady
WITH MOUSTACHE STRAWS

YOU WILL NEED

30ml vodka

15ml gin

15ml triple sec

60ml pineapple juice

15ml passion fruit juice

15ml fresh lime juice

ice-cubes

bitters

soda water

WELL I NEVER, A LADY, WITH A BEARD? No, it is not a comedy sketch, it is in fact a rather splendid cocktail. With such a great name it just wouldn't be the same without serving it with these easy straws; just cut the moustache shapes below out of black card and use dots of glue to stick them to straws.

Pour the vodka, gin, triple sec and all the fruit juices into a cocktail shaker containing ice. Shake vigorously and strain into a tall, iced pilsner glass. Add a dash of bitters and top with some soda water. Serve with a moustache straw.

Moustache
TEMPLATES

MAKES 1 GLASS

Wild HANNAH

1 wild hibiscus flower, in rose syrup
1 tsp rose syrup from the jar
15ml crème de cassis
15ml elderflower liqueur
champagne
fresh figs, halved

Place the hibiscus flower in a champagne flute and add the syrup, crème de cassis and the elderflower. Top with some champagne, place a halved fig on the edge of the glass and serve.

NO, THIS DRINK ISN'T FROM THE WILD WEST!
This heavenly drink has become my firm favourite and a signature offering at all of my GNI. Topped with champagne, you are going to love this pretty concoction.

MAKES 1
GLASS

Templates

STRAW, UMBRELLA AND LEMON

For cocktail
invitation, p.9

Enlarge by 150%

TOP

For skirt invitation, p.9

4.5cm

7cm

6cm

17cm

SHOE

For shoe invitation, p.8

Enlarge by 150%

cut on fold

13cm

13cm

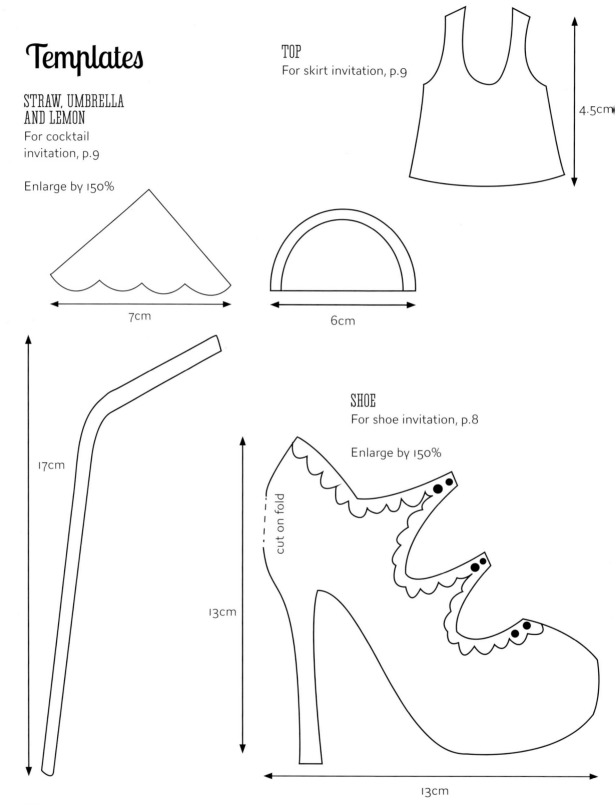

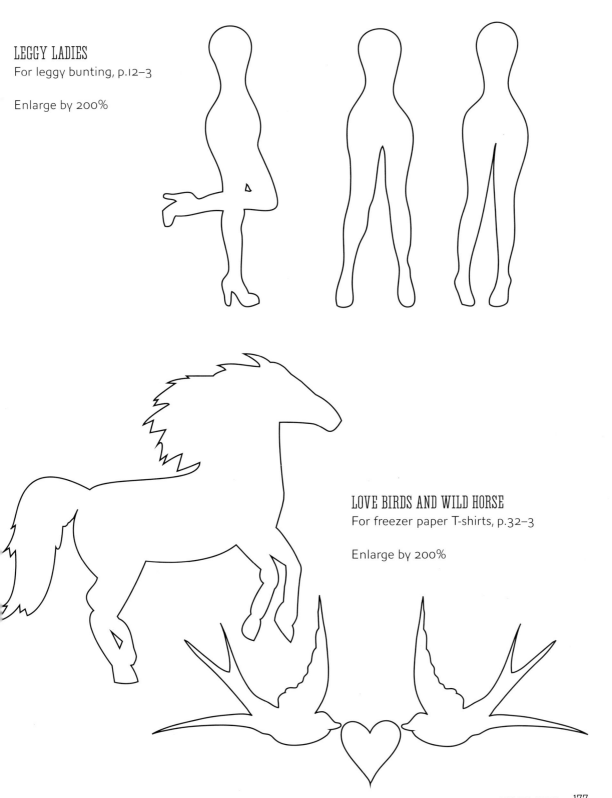

LEGGY LADIES
For leggy bunting, p.12–3

Enlarge by 200%

LOVE BIRDS AND WILD HORSE
For freezer paper T-shirts, p.32–3

Enlarge by 200%

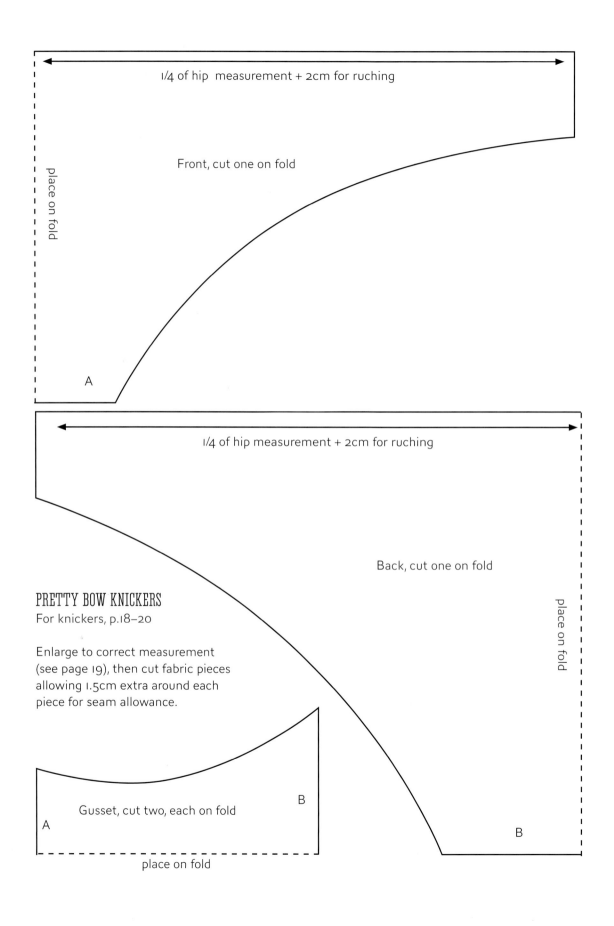

1/4 of hip measurement + 2cm for ruching

place on fold

Front, cut one on fold

A

1/4 of hip measurement + 2cm for ruching

Back, cut one on fold

place on fold

PRETTY BOW KNICKERS
For knickers, p.18–20

Enlarge to correct measurement
(see page 19), then cut fabric pieces
allowing 1.5cm extra around each
piece for seam allowance.

B

Gusset, cut two, each on fold

A

B

place on fold

TWO ROSES AND PIN-UP GIRL
For tea towel, p.28–30

Enlarge by 150%

BIRD, STAR AND BUTTERFLY EMBROIDERY
For simple sewn skirt, p.34–37

Enlarge by 120%

SKULL AND ROSES EMBROIDERY
For simple sewn skirt, p.34–37

PHOTOBOOTH PIECES
For photo booth, p.38–9

Enlarge by 400%

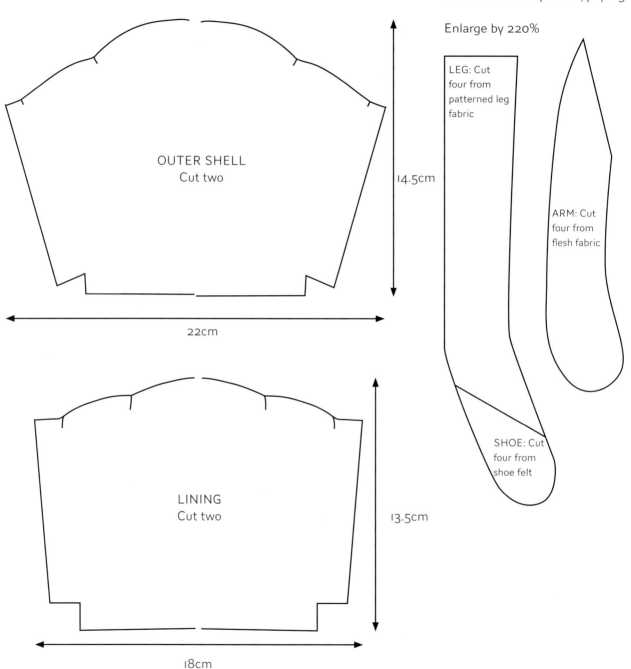

CLUTCH BAG PIECES
For cute clutch bag, p.46–7

Enlarge by 200%

ARM AND LEG
For mini-me doll pattern, p.48–51

Enlarge by 220%

OUTER SHELL
Cut two

14.5cm

22cm

LEG: Cut
four from
patterned leg
fabric

ARM: Cut
four from
flesh fabric

LINING
Cut two

13.5cm

SHOE: Cut
four from
shoe felt

18cm

R, HEAD AND BODY
mini-me doll pattern, p.48–51

arge by 220%

HAIR: Cut
one from
hair felt

BACK OF HEAD:
Cut one from
hair felt and one
from flesh fabric

COLLAR: Cut
two from
collar felt

BODY: Cut
two from
patterened
body fabric

SILHOUETTE SHOES, BOWS AND BUTTERFLIES
For silhouette lampshades, p.54–5

Enlarge by 200% (or in various sizes)

MASK
For butterfly mask, p.68–9

Enlarge by 220%

20cm

28cm

LEGGY TOPPER
For cake, p.130–1

Directory

CRAFT MATERIALS

Baker Ross
The place to buy cheap fabric paint, brushes and glue.

2–3 Forest Works
Forest Road
Walthamstow
London E17 6JF
0844 576 8922
www.bakerross.co.uk

Beads and Crystals
The company sells HotFix Crystals as well as glue on crystals.

01926 889966
www.beadsandcrystals.co.uk

Covent Garden Bead Shop
Stocks a huge selection of beads, including gemstones, semi-precious beads, chains and bead kits.

21a Tower Street
Covent Garden
London WC2H 9NS
020 7240 0931
www.beadworks.co.uk

The Eternal Maker
This is a great website to order from. They sell gorgeous coloured felt as well as lovely purse clasps.

01243 788174
www.eternalmaker.com

Fabric UK
You can order sample sizes of the pastel-coloured leatherettes from here, more than enough to make a selection of bunting necklaces.

0121 359 2349
www.fabricuk.com

The Hanging Lantern Company
Stocks an amazing selection of paper lanterns in every possible colour.

0845 465 5585
www.hanginglanterns.co.uk

HobbyCraft
The place to buy scrapbook paper, glue and other general craft supplies.

01202 596 100
www.hobbycraft.co.uk

The Cloth House
A shop that is definitely worth a visit as it sells a great selection of top quality fabrics.

47 & 98 Berwick Street
London W1F OQJ
020 7437 5155
www.clothhouse.com

Liberty
Sells a variety of beautiful printed silks.

Great Marlborough Street
London W1B 5AH
020 7734 1234
www.liberty.co.uk

Jane Means Ribbons
An unimaginable selection of every ribbon you could ever wish for!

01522 522 544
www.janemeans.com

JK Clothing
A place to bulk buy white tea towels.

www.jkclothing.co.uk

COOKING SUPPLIES

Lakeland
Perfect for every possible piece of cooking equipment, from bamboo skewers to a variety of cake tins.

015394 88100
www.lakeland.co.uk

Totally Sugar Crafts
Brilliant selection of everything you could need for cake decoration, from piping nozzles to glitter.

www.totallysugarcrafts.co.uk

COCKTAIL INGREDIENTS

The Cooking Source
Sells delicious Wild Hibiscus Flowers in syrup.

www.thecookingsource.co.uk

The Drink Shop
For cherries with stems, which are harder to find than you may think!

www.thedrinkshop.com

MAKE-UP & HAIR SPONSORED PRODUCTS

Mac
www.maccosmetics.co.uk

Chanel
www.chanel.com

Laura Mercier
www.lauramercier.com

Bumble and Bumble
www.bumbleandbumble.co.uk

OPI
www.opi.com

Index

Editorial Director Jane O'Shea
Creative Director Helen Lewis
Commissioning Editor Lisa Pendreigh
Created by Hannah Read-Baldrey
Editor Louise McKeever
Designer Claire Peters
Still Life Photography Verity Welstead
Portrait Photography Tiffany Mumford
Make-up Design Fiona Fletcher
Nail Design Lucy Pearson
Make-up Nina Sagri
Hair and Make-up Assistant Melanie Menendez
Production Director Vincent Smith
Production Controller Sasha Taylor

Quadrille
craft

www.quadrillecraft.co.uk

First published in 2013 by
Quadrille Publishing Ltd
Alhambra House
27–31 Charing Cross Road
London WC2H 0LS
www.quadrille.co.uk

Text, project designs & artwork © 2013 Hannah Read-Baldrey
Photography © 2013 Tiffany Mumford & Verity Welstead
Design & layout © 2013 Quadrille Publishing Ltd

British Library Cataloguing-in-Publication Data
A catalogue record for this book is available from the British Library.

ISBN: 978 184949 265 2

Printed in China.

ACKNOWLEDGEMENTS

Thank you to all the women who took part in the making of this book – Rebecca, Flora, Rachael, Jessica, Alison (Carl) and Salma – thank you so much for agreeing to be my supermodels and for your input into the serious debate over the top 20 Chick Flicks! Verity, thank you for your wonderful photographs, your light-hearted humour and catchphrase compliments on my cooking ("Oh I shouldn't, oh but it is good…") are always appreciated! Tiffany thank you for the beautiful pictures, the girls will have lovely keepsakes. Claire, Louise, Lisa and Jane, for seeing the potential in the idea and helping me along the journey, as always your support has been amazing. Fiona for being the fabulous make-up artist and friend and Lucy for your ingenious nail art, you've got us all addicted now! Carole and Paul, thank you for so generously lending me your gorgeous home to shoot in. Christine for being my design guru. Mum, for your famous Slug Cake recipe, Brendan, my husbear, who puts up with all sorts of shoots in our home with barely a growl!

GOODIE BAG

No, goodie bags are not just for kids! Everyone will want to take home their special craft make, a cupcake or two and even a picture of themselves dressed up in a comedy moustache! Whatever your guests go home with, you will know that they had a fabulous time and all that's left to do is to decide who is going to host the next Girls' Night In!